To Mark —

On the occasion of his

40th. Birthday.

With my love and

very best wishes —

Dad x

19 . 12 . 98 .

From Arlott to Aggers

40 YEARS

of

TEST MATCH SPECIAL

Veuve Clicquot champagne has had a close association with TEST MATCH SPECIAL over the past six years through the Brian Johnston Champagne Moment and, while this book is not a collection of the Champagne Moments chosen by the TMS team at matches over the years, it does reflect the same theme.

As followers of the programme will be aware, the Brian Johnston Champagne Moment is awarded to the player who produces the most memorable moment of the match – the moment which makes you want to open a bottle of Veuve Clicquot in celebration not just of a great piece of cricket but of the spirit of the game. The connection is a natural one and we are delighted to have been associated with TEST MATCH SPECIAL.

In *From Arlott to Aggers* the contributors regale us with tales of their favourite moments in the commentary box as well as on the field. There have been so many special moments over the years that it will be very interesting to see what each contributor picks out as their outstanding moment – and it will certainly provide a fascinating collection of entertaining stories.

So many people have been involved with TMS over the last 40 years, both behind the scenes and behind the microphone, that it would be impossible to mention them all. Instead I would like to offer a collective thank you to you all on behalf of the millions of listeners for all the joy you have brought to us over the years and will, I am sure, continue to do so for many years to come.

Congratulations, TEST MATCH SPECIAL, on 40 wonderful years, and I raise a glass of Veuve Clicquot to you all.

With best wishes,

From Arlott to Aggers

40

Y E A R S

of

TEST MATCH SPECIAL

ANDRE
DEUTSCH

'And there's a pigeon on the pitch...'

Edited by
PETER BAXTER AND PHIL McNEILL

Designed by
ROB KELLAND

With thanks to:
Dave Crowe and all at DC Publications, for helping to set up the Listeners' Poll;
Catherine McNeill, for inputting mountains of copy and counting the Listeners' Poll;
Mark Goldsmith at Allsport, for endless photo research;
and especially to the hundreds of TMS listeners who sent in their Champagne Moments.

First published in Great Britain in 1997 by André Deutsch Ltd
106 Great Russell Street, London WC1B 3LJ
www.vci.co.uk

André Deutsch is a subsidiary of VCI plc

Copyright © DC Publications 1997

'Test Match Special' is a trade mark of the BBC
Based on the BBC Series 'Test Match Special'

A catalogue record for this title is available from the British Library

ISBN 0 233 99215 4

Printed and bound in Great Britain
by Butler & Tanner, Frome and London

· CONTENTS ·

6 **Foreword by Sir Colin Cowdrey**

8 THE TEST MATCH SPECIAL STORY
By Peter Baxter

12 *Champagne Moments*

14 THE TEST MATCH SPECIAL DECADES
Five TMS commentators recall the events that have shaped the world's greatest game.
By Trevor Bailey, Henry Blofeld, Christopher Martin-Jenkins, Vic Marks and Chris Cowdrey

46 *Champagne Moments*

48 A DAY IN THE COMMENTARY BOX
A peep behind the scenes with Aggers, Blowers, The Bearded Wonder and all. By David Cavanagh

54 TEST MATCH SPECIAL LISTENERS' POLL
The people's choice of Best Commentator Ever, Best Brain in the Box, Best Sense of Humour...
Plus the listeners' Favourite Cricketer from 40 years of TMS

56 JOHN AND JOHNNERS
A tribute to John Arlott and Brian Johnston. By Sir Tim Rice

60 *Champagne Moments*

62 TEST MATCH SPECIAL BALL BY BALL
Matches that made history since 1957. By Trevor Bailey, Robert Hudson, Fred Trueman,
Bryan Waddle, Mike Selvey, Henry Blofeld, Peter Baxter, Graeme Fowler, Tony Cozier, Vic Marks,
Christopher Martin-Jenkins, Gerald de Kock, David Lloyd, Jonathan Agnew and Chris Cowdrey.
Including, on page 81, Bill Frindall's scorecard for Headingley '81

104 *Champagne Moments*

106 DREAM TEAMS
TMS experts choose their World XI from the past 40 years

116 *Champagne Moments*

118 TMS IN 2037
The next 40 years of cricket broadcasting. By Jonathan Agnew

Send more lozenges, they have to talk all day!

by Sir Colin Cowdrey

here were three special reasons to remember the First Test Match against West Indies at Edgbaston in 1957. Warwickshire had not staged a Test Match since 1929 and, under the direction of their much loved Secretary, Leslie Deakins, it proved to be a well-appointed venue for Test cricket.

This match also marked the start of TEST MATCH SPECIAL, a broadcasting team committed to providing ball-by-ball commentary on the whole match.

I remember so clearly the England team greeting them during our practice session on the Wednesday afternoon – John Arlott, Rex Alston, distinguished journalist and former Yorkshire and England bowler Bill Bowes and, from the West Indies, Kenneth Ablack. At the time, the thought of them sitting trapped in their little broadcasting box seven hours a day, having to watch every ball bowled, being fed and watered in their hutch, seemed a tough assignment. With much merriment we presented a few tins of throat lozenges each morning to the box, hoping that they would have the stamina to survive.

Little did we realise that this new idea would become established so quickly and that TEST MATCH SPECIAL would grow into a national institution.

It turned out to be an extraordinary match. Little Sonny Ramadhin was the unfathomable mystery bowler, possibly a more fearsome ogre in prospect than Shane Warne today. We had heard that if we unleashed an

attack upon him from the start, he might fold and disappear from view. We forged a plan to destroy him.

Having won the toss on a lovely batting pitch, we set about him. The plan appeared to work … except that we kept losing wickets. We scored at a tremendous pace, but were all out for 186 before tea, Ramadhin seven for 49.

With relative comfort, West Indies built a lead of 288 by Saturday afternoon. It looked as if the new TEST MATCH SPECIAL broadcasting team might enjoy a shortened day on the Monday and a complete day off on Tuesday.

Starting on Monday at 102 for two, I joined Peter May just before midday and we put on 411 together, closing soon after 2.30 on the Tuesday. Peter May declared a little while later and, somewhat breathless, the players, the crowd, the Press box and the broadcasters watched on in astonishment as West Indies battled to survive at 72 for seven when stumps were drawn.

Edgbaston had provided an historic cricket occasion, and the TEST MATCH SPECIAL concept had been given a marvellous send-off.

Colin Cowdrey

'Don't miss a ball, we broadcast them all'

BY Peter Baxter

'Cricket is one of the slowest games in the world.' So declared the *Radio Times* in 1927, and that in a build-up for the first cricket outside broadcast in England. It dismissed the idea of running commentary as impossible. I often wonder if that unnamed writer was around thirty years later when TEST MATCH SPECIAL was launched, carrying running commentary throughout the day, every day.

On 14 May 1927 Essex were playing the New Zealanders at Leyton. The BBC, following on the winter's successes in describing rugby and soccer matches, decided to try cricket. After all, the Australians had already done it. They had even tried the running description of play which the BBC said was impossible. On this particular experimental Saturday, though, the Rev. Frank Gillingham, a fine Essex batsman at the end of his first-class career, was given a microphone in the pavilion and at certain fixed times, during a programme otherwise composed of waltzes and foxtrots, he gave 'accounts of the state of the game'.

The newspapers that thought these humble beginnings to cricket commentary worthy of note were divided in their opinions as to its success, although the *Western Daily Press* did, while largely condemning the idea as ludicrous, identify the fact that a good commentator was as important as the quality of the game. When five-minute descriptions of play from a Roses match were proposed a few weeks later, Neville Cardus, no less – a man who might have made the sort of attritional cricket he anticipated sound amusing and even interesting – wrote a piece of satire taking the mickey out of the whole idea.

Over the next ten years a few people dipped their toes in the commentary waters. Sir Pelham Warner, a legendary player and administrator but no natural broadcaster, did commentaries, reports and cricket 'talks'. Teddy Wakelam had been the pioneer of rugby commentary and so, knowing something of the game, was asked to try his skill at describing cricket in action.

His experience at The Oval in August 1927 was an unhappy one on a dull day's play between Surrey and Middlesex. Unfortunately for the immediate future of this new art, Wakelam was considered something of a messiah in outside broadcasting and so his opinion that

Early fans of TEST MATCH SPECIAL: Tony Lock's wife and sons are up early to listen in to commentary from the 1958 Test in Brisbane. Young Richard and Graeme look pretty excited considering Dad took only one wicket in the match and scored just six runs! The signed photo on the radio shows Lock with Alec Bedser, Jim Laker and Peter May

the game was indeed impossible to commentate on remained the official BBC view for nearly a decade.

The crucial teaming-up that set cricket on its way to becoming the pre-eminent sport for radio commentary came in the Thirties with the arrival of the former lawyer Seymour de Lotbinière (known to generations in the BBC as 'Lobby') as Head of Outside Broadcasts together with a man who could carry out his ideas for commentary – Howard Marshall.

Marshall was a trained journalist who had already, in his early thirties, been Assistant News Editor at the BBC and would go on to be the top outside broadcast commentator, covering the Coronation of George VI and the D-Day landings. But his lasting legacy to broadcasting

is the art of ball-by-ball commentary. The first recording of cricket commentary saved in the BBC archives is Marshall's description of the 1934 Test at Lord's, when Hedley Verity spun England to an innings victory over Australia. The occasional commentaries from that series captured the nation's imagination and started to give it a thirst for more. That Lord's Test, as Marshall desperately tried to keep track while Verity took 14 wickets for 80 runs on the third day, had the side effect of highlighting the commentator's need for a scorer. Arthur Wrigley was appointed for the next Test. The use of an expert summariser, though, was still in the future.

Cricket commentary probably truly entered the national culture with Howard Marshall's description of Len Hutton's

Brian Johnston, John Arlott and Alan McGilvray – three greats of cricket commentary who are sadly no longer with us

great innings at The Oval in 1938. His words, delivered in his rich, full-bodied, measured tones, still live in the memories of the pre-war listeners who heard him describe Hutton pass Bradman's record for an Anglo-Australian Test Match.

'*The total – Hutton's total 332. It sounds like the total of the whole side. The England total 707 for five and the gasometer sinking lower and lower. Here's Fleetwood-Smith again to Hutton. Hutton hits him. Oh, beautiful stroke! There's the record...*'

That same year, E. W. Swanton was due to go on tour with MCC to South Africa on behalf of the *Evening Standard*. He approached the BBC to see if he might combine his newspaper work with some broadcasts on the series. After a baptism of fire at The Oval for a county match when, thanks to rain elsewhere, he had to talk for a straight half-hour including the ten-minute change of innings without the aid of either a scorer or a summariser, he was duly commissioned and did periods of commentary which included that gift for a commentator, a hat-trick – this by Tom Goddard on Boxing Day.

The following summer, 1939, the BBC had agreed with the West Indian stations to broadcast to them every ball of the Test Matches which the West Indies were to play in England and so Swanton joined Howard Marshall and another eminent BBC broadcaster, Michael Standing, to do that. But while listeners in Jamaica and Barbados heard the entire match, those in England still only received periods of commentary.

Then came the Second World War and with it the arrival at the BBC of a former schoolmaster, appointed now as billeting officer. His name was Rex Alston and he did not stay long in that administrative role, doing his first commentary on a wartime cricket match and then helping Howard Marshall with the coverage of the Victory Tests in 1946.

That year brought a new recruit to cricket commentary, when the BBC's Eastern Service asked its recently appointed poetry producer to follow the Indian touring team round. The poetry wallah's prose, delivered in a rolling Hampshire brogue, so captivated his sub-continental audience that he was asked to continue. His name was John Arlott.

So, for the arrival of Bradman's Australians in 1948, the BBC had a team to do full commentary – but only for Australia, although the BBC's periods of joining that commentary were becoming more extensive. Alston, Arlott and Swanton were joined by the Australian Broadcasting Commission's Alan McGilvray. By that time, too, the commentators had some expert opinion to call on. In that 1948 series and several others it was Arthur Gilligan, former captain of Sussex and England.

Commentary periods were now accepted – although, as they were not of a complete day's play, crucial moments were missed. Still, John Arlott's description of Bradman's last innings in 1948, Rex Alston's of the West Indies' historic Lord's victory in 1950, Bernie Kerr of the ABC at The Oval in 1953 when England won back the Ashes, and Arlott again at Old Trafford in 1956 watching Laker take his 19th wicket were all events brought into people's homes. Now, for the start of the 1957 series with the West Indies in England, came the crucial move that established ball-by-ball commentary for an entire Test Match.

Commentary periods had previously been mainly on the Light Programme (now Radio 2) and sometimes also switched to the Home Service (Radio 4). Now, by using the Third Network (Radio 3) as well, the BBC was able to publish with its billing in the *Radio Times* the slogan 'Don't miss a ball, we broadcast them all' – a boast it was able to continue until 1994.

And to accompany the new service came a new name: TEST MATCH SPECIAL.

It was a historic and dramatic Test Match for the new programme's launch, too, recalled elsewhere in this book by Trevor Bailey. The commentators at Edgbaston, while they must have been relieved to know that they were broadcasting the whole day's play, even though listeners had to hop around the networks to hear it, probably had no idea of what an institution they were starting.

The team was Rex Alston, John Arlott and the West Indian Ken Ablack, with expert comments from Bill Bowes and Gerry Gomez and a close-of-summary by E. W. Swanton. The producer then was Michael Tuke-Hastings, who remained in that role until I took over in

1973. Over the next few years came Robert Hudson, the model commentator, Alan Gibson, the academic crafter of words, Neil Durden-Smith and Don Mosey.

But surely the biggest influence on the flavour of TEST MATCH SPECIAL was the decision by BBC Television in 1970 to dispense with the services of Brian Johnston. He was elevated to the radio commentary and it is surely no coincidence that the popularity of the programme really took off in the Seventies. Some listeners may have regretted the sense of irreverence that Johnners brought to the commentary box with his boyish japes and chocolate cakes, but it is arguable that Brian's wide appeal (and undisputed love of cricket) introduced a new audience to the erudite talents of John Arlott.

The Seventies also saw the arrival of two of today's pillars of commentary, Henry Blofeld and Christopher Martin-Jenkins, who would join Johnston and Mosey to see the programme through the Eighties. A rare but welcome shot of new blood came in 1991 with the arrival of the former England fast bowler Jonathan Agnew. Expert summarisers have, of necessity, changed more frequently, but few have moved on untouched by their time as part of the TMS family.

Contrary to the fears of that 1927 *Radio Times* previewer, the very slowness of cricket has proved to be its greatest asset on radio. The intervals between deliveries allow time for description and analysis that a more frenetic sport cannot afford. Even the best football commentators do not have breathing space among the hurly-burly of the action to reflect on players' skills and characters... let alone a No. 12 bus passing down the Harleyford Road.

In Brian Johnston's words, *Test Match Special* is 'like a group of friends at a cricket match. We sit together, swap jokes, and if someone has a good tale to tell he's

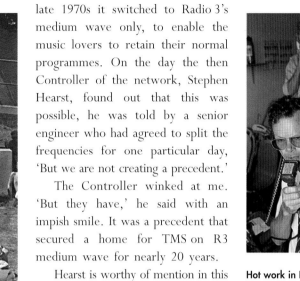

'The very slowness of cricket has turned out to be its greatest asset on radio'

encouraged to tell it. But we *are* professionals and, most importantly, we all think that cricket is fun.' Thus the slowest of sports has become, on radio, the most enduringly popular.

In 1963 the use of the Light Programme was dropped and TEST MATCH SPECIAL started 29 years of continuous commentary on the Third Network and Radio 3. In the late 1970s it switched to Radio 3's medium wave only, to enable the music lovers to retain their normal programmes. On the day the then Controller of the network, Stephen Hearst, found out that this was possible, he was told by a senior engineer who had agreed to split the frequencies for one particular day, 'But we are not creating a precedent.'

The Controller winked at me. 'But they have,' he said with an impish smile. It was a precedent that secured a home for TMS on R3 medium wave for nearly 20 years.

Hearst is worthy of mention in this story. Born in Austria, with no background of cricket, he nevertheless saw the cultural place of this strange art form of cricket commentary and would sit in my office to discuss the word selection of John Arlott or the opinions of Fred Trueman or even the jokes of Brian Johnston. The balance of the characters of the team intrigued him and he was always delighted to be able to step out of Broadcasting House in the summer and find people in the street listening to his network on transistor radios.

He knew, though, as his successors on all networks have found, especially since the 1992 Broadcasting Act removed two wavelengths from the BBC, that TEST MATCH SPECIAL is a problem for programme planners. It takes up too much of the day to be comfortably assimilated. Sadly, for the time being at least, we can no longer say: 'Don't miss a ball, we broadcast them all.'

Hot work in Barbados, 1990, but the CMJ tie stays crisply in place. Left: Even on the Hill at the SCG, Blowers makes friends wherever he goes

Champagne Moments

My Champagne Moment is the last of Jim Laker's 19 wickets in a Test Match – Old Trafford, 31 July 1956. It was truly unbelievable and it has not been paralleled anywhere by bat or ball. Apart from this great historic cricket feat, it encouraged me to listen to every ball of the commentary in case I missed something – and I have done so ever since, even here in Ireland.

– David Rose, Dublin

My Champagne Moment: Listening to Henry Blofeld and Don Mosey (at least one of whom had got out of bed on the wrong side) bickering about whether a feature on the horizon was the minaret of a mosque, or not – which they found much more interesting than the game!

– Brian Beard, Biggin Hill, Kent

ROBERT HUDSON'S CHAMPAGNE MOMENT

A sting in the tale

On TMS I loved to fiddle with the rubber bands used by scorer Arthur Wrigley to bind his score-sheets. Once I overdid it – and the lethal missile shot across the box and hit Freddie Brown on the ear. He thought he'd been stung by a wasp, and his yelp was heard all over the world.

DAVID LLOYD'S CHAMPAGNE MOMENT

The stylist supreme

David Gower's four through cover against Pakistan to go past Geoffrey Boycott as England's top run-getter.

My Champagne Moment was Boycott's 100th century. We were on the road from the motorway to Tewkesbury. I recall the elation as clearly as I remember where I was when I heard that Kennedy had been shot.

– Jack Porter, Sheffield

The removal of Ray Bright's middle stump by Bob Willis to win the 1981 Headingley Test Match. Even my wife, on whose list of interests cricket comes some way below the European Haddock Classification regulations, was gripped. The exultation as that middle stump went over still lives with me. (NB: This only narrowly beat into second place the moment during 1995 when Jonathan Agnew was sprayed with wasp repellent.)

– David Lees, Shepherds Bush, London

TEST MATCH SPECIAL
Quiz
• THE FIFTIES •

1 In Test Match Special's first season, Peter Loader took a Test Match hat-trick. Who were his three victims?

Answer on page 120

As an MCC Pavilion steward at Lord's for some 14 years, and Senior Steward in the Pavilion for four years, I write from the inside of the fence! The Champagne Moment for us came on the first day of the Test Matches at Lord's.

Summer didn't arrive till then, when the commentators drifted in. Whatever the pressures, always ready to stop and chat before the ascent to the heights of the commentary box.

Then the chocolate cakes and goodies would have to be taken up to the box. One of the stewards suggested we rename the Commentary Box the Calorie Box. Brian Johnston said we had a nerve, because he said he hadn't seen a Pavilion steward under 14 stone in weight for years.

We couldn't meet a more pleasant group and it reflected in their commentaries. The best informed, never a dull moment, and at times the very best of British vaudeville.
— *Jim Radcliffe, London NW3*

My Champagne Moment is from 1978: David Gower caressing his first ball in Test cricket for four – and John Arlott's purring reaction: 'What a princely entry! This boy has class.'
— *Neil Phillips, Richmond, Surrey*

CHRISTOPHER MARTIN-JENKINS'S
CHAMPAGNE MOMENT

Defeated by a taxi driver

How in heaven do you sort out one Champagne Moment on the field of play? Derek Randall turning a cartwheel after taking the catch which won England the Ashes in 1977... The six which took Ian Botham to his second hundred in three Tests against Australia in 1981... Devon Malcolm bursting through Hansie Cronje's defence on the way to nine wickets at The Oval... No, I shall go for a distant memory off the field.

Christmas in India in 1976-7. The radio phone-in was in its infancy then, but the BBC wanted me to get England captain Tony Greig to a studio in a far-off hill station in Assam to talk to fans at home. A phone call live on air from Gauhati to London? Mad! But the lines were booked, so I dutifully persuaded Greig into a taxi and said to the driver: 'Please take us to All India Radio.'

'Ullindia?' he asked with a frown.
'Yes please, All India.'
'Acha. Ullindia. Please get in.'

We did, and he drove off into a misty night. I thought the studio was on the fringe of the city but we had been going 45 minutes when I leaned forward to check. 'All India soon?'

'Acha,' he replied with a confident waggle of the head. 'Ullindia.'

Sure enough, five minutes later he pulled up in triumph at some large wrought-iron gates. On the front was a noticeboard painted in huge, unmistakable letters: Oil India Ltd.

I vividly remember listening to the first day of the Calcutta Test in 1992-3.

The sound quality was terrible; it was difficult to separate the chanting crowd from the hiss and crackle; the cricket was bad; the team behaving more like the retreat from Kabul than honed athletes...

The overall effect, on an icy, dark morning in England, was magical and bracing, as if listening to familiar voices from another galaxy.
— *Lutgen Mentz, London W4*

My Champagne Moment goes back to 1963, England v West Indies at Lord's, the Second Test Match. On the last day, England at 116 for three needed 118 runs to win in 200 minutes.

Working in an office in the City of London, we listened on a small portable radio. Five o'clock was the time to go home, but most of the staff stayed behind until the last dramatic moments just before 6pm, when Cowdrey with one arm in plaster came out to bat.

Luckily he did not have to face a ball as Allen played the last two balls and a draw was the result.
— *R. W. Morfill, St Paul's Cray, Kent*

· The Fifties ·

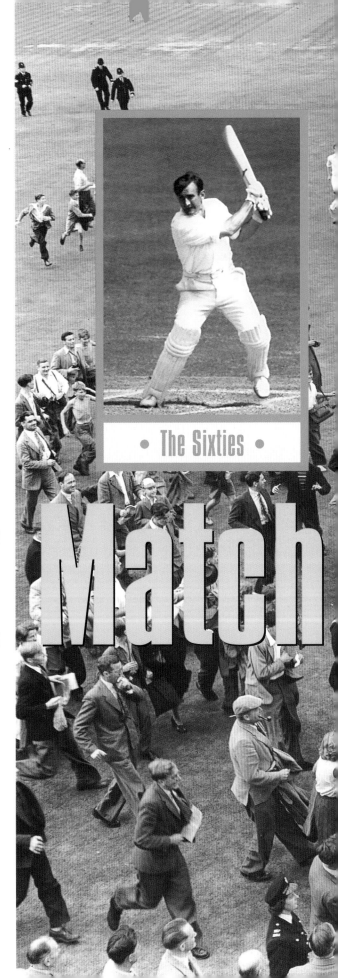

· The Sixties ·

The Test Match

From Brylcreem boys to Cellphone superstars,
from MCC majors to the Barmy Army.
How cricket became a whole new ball game

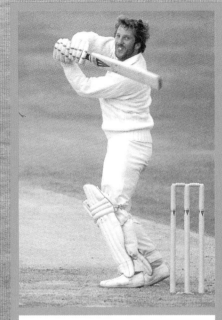

• The Seventies •

• The Eighties •

• The Nineties •

Special Decades

From left: Jim Laker,
Ted Dexter, Alan Knott,
Ian Botham, Graham Gooch

The Fifties

COMPTON AND EDRICH, TRUEMAN AND STATHAM, LAKER AND LOCK...
ONE OF THE STARS OF A GILDED ERA RECALLS THE PLAYERS AND
TECHNIQUES THAT MADE ENGLAND UNOFFICIAL WORLD CHAMPIONS

BY
Trevor Bailey

The renaissance of English cricket occurred during what in modern parlance might be termed the Fab Fifties. It stemmed from several factors, the most important being the arrival of a number of high-class home-grown cricketers after the Second World War. Until then England, apart from Alec Bedser and Godfrey Evans, had had to rely on mainly pre-war players. Although this policy had proved sufficient against India and South Africa, it had not worked against either Australia or the rapidly improving West Indies.

This fresh influx of exciting new talent was respons-ible for our national team in the mid-Fifties becoming the unofficial world champions until 1959, when what appeared to be an exceptionally strong team was destroyed by Australia. Our Selectors then decided to dismantle and rebuild, which unfortunately was not noticeably successful, and we have never been able to reclaim that title. At this moment we must lie sixth in order of merit among the Test-playing nations.

England's success in the Fifties was mainly due to a powerful and well-balanced attack, which enabled us to dismiss the opposition twice on all types of pitch. The most decisive figures in Test cricket are usually the pace bowlers, though in the Fifties and Sixties this applied more overseas than in England. We had Frank Tyson, the fastest bowler in the world; Fred Trueman, the best fast bowler England has produced; Brian Statham, just about the most accurate fast bowler ever; and Alec Bedser, the greatest fast medium since the war – while Peter Loader, who would surely have commanded a regular place in any other post-war national team, supplied the back-up.

The spin department was also crammed with quite exceptional talent (and spinners, like pacemen, tend to be more effective in tandem). Jim Laker was surely the best off-spinner in the history of the game, Bob Appleyard was possibly the best dual-purpose English Test bowler, Roy Tattersall was true international calibre, Tony Lock and Johnny Wardle were world-class left-armers in their very different ways, while Fred Titmus and Ray Illingworth were in the process of establishing themselves in the top flight.

The England batting was not quite so impressive, but

Three lions on their chests – a classic England team line-up for the 1953 Oval Test against Australia. Back row, from left: Trevor Bailey, Peter May, Tom Graveney, Jim Laker, Tony Lock, Johnny Wardle and Fred Trueman. Front: Bill Edrich, Alec Bedser, Len Hutton, Denis Compton and Godfrey Evans

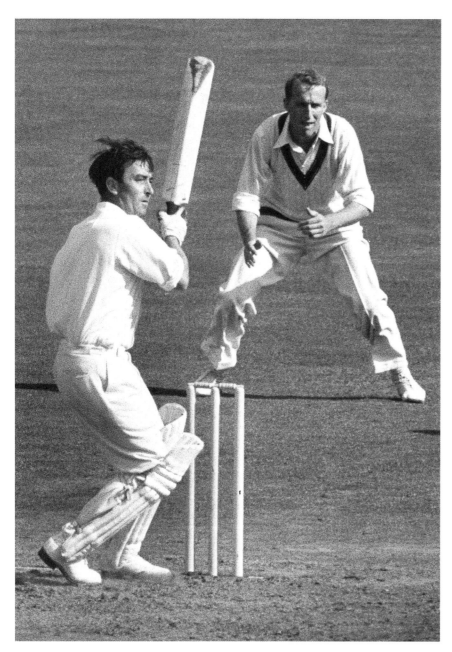

beat South Africa and the West Indies and regain the Ashes after an absence of 19 years, but I believe it meant rather more to us than it does now, albeit not in terms of money. We were all representing the country where we had learned the game and for which many players and spectators had fought a bloody war. As a result, although we played our cricket very hard, and were probably too ruthless on occasions, it was still a game which contained laughter. There was certainly no sledging. Nobody ever swore at me to my face – and there were occasions when this was undoubtedly justified.

It was also a wonderful era for county cricket, which drew large, well-behaved and very enthusiastic crowds, and the tourists match was a highlight of the summer.

There have never been so many outstanding English players since then on the county circuit. The championship was dominated by Surrey, which was hardly surprising when one considers that their attack contained Alec Bedser, Loader, Laker and Lock, with Eric Bedser and their very forceful leader Stuart Surridge in support. Their closest rivals, Yorkshire, also possessed a formidable line-up with Trueman, Appleyard, Wardle and Illingworth, plus Brian Close. This should have been a bonus for our Selectors, because anyone who regularly scored runs against either county must

Denis Compton, original Brylcreem boy, in action against Australia in 1953. Right: Len Hutton recalls past duels with a retired Don Bradman, also in '53

it did contain four very high-class performers in Peter May, Colin Cowdrey, Tom Graveney and Ted Dexter, with Ken Barrington beginning to express his enormous talent.

There was something very special about playing for England in the Fifties, not only because we managed to

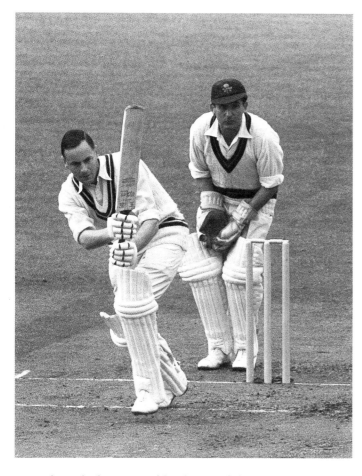

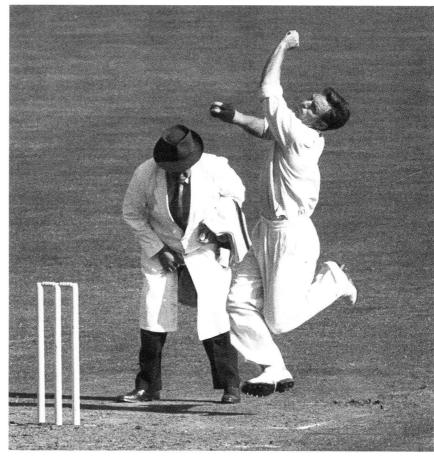

have had a reasonable chance of doing well in a Test.

For me one of the most fascinating features of the Fifties was the excellent technique displayed by so many of the pre-war batsman. Have we ever discovered at the same time four better young players than Hutton, Denis Compton, Bill Edrich and Joe Hardstaff? What other records would they have broken, but for those missing years? I especially treasure the memory of Len Hutton batting on a 'sticky'.

However, it would be wrong to imagine that it was all sweetness and light in the Fifties. After all, we did deliberately dispatch the occasional beamer and a new, more cynical thinking had begun to creep into the game. Many of the pre-war ideas were queried and dismissed. For example, was it sensible to take a wrist spinner to Australia, simply because he was one, instead of selecting

an off-spinner who was a much better bowler? Field placings became far more imaginative. The idea that bowlers had set fields which were seldom changed was abandoned. Having bowled on that day when Australia scored 721 runs, I would never permit a batting massacre on that scale to occur again. Although captains frequently set ultra attacking fields, they quickly reverted to the defensive when their opponents threatened to dominate. They also appreciated that a run-saving field could sometimes provide a counter-attack by enticing the batsmen to take chances, while another tactic to reduce the run rate was simply to slow the over rate.

There was nothing new about leg theory, but in the Fifties its main objective was to slow the run rate by using quick bowlers aiming at and outside the leg stump. This reduced the normal scoring arc by fifty per cent, as

Two great adversaries of the Fifties – Peter May, who scored 1,566 runs against Australia, and Ray Lindwall, who took 114 wickets against England

few batsmen had either the skill or ingenuity to hit the ball through the off side from there. Although it was feasible to improvise for a short period against this form of bowling, I never encountered a batsman who was able to score quickly against it for any length of time. The players themselves recognised this fact and tacitly abandoned what had been an interesting ploy, which I had first employed as an experiment in Australia in 1950.

Years later the administrators introduced a new law which, by reducing the number of on-side fielders to five (of whom only two could be stationed behind the popping crease), destroyed this tactic. Sadly, this was a serious handicap for in-swing and off-spin bowlers when they were attacking.

Bowlers with doubtful arm actions have been around since the game began, but in the Fifties there was an explosion of them. The two most common types are the finger spinner and the paceman. It is much easier for a finger spinner to make the ball break by throwing it than by bowling it with a straight arm. In the Fifties Tony Lock

The author lives up to his Fifties nickname of Barnacle Bailey, practising a meticulous straight bat during the MCC tour of Australia in 1955

'Many players and spectators had fought a
bloody war. We played hard, but it was still
a game which contained laughter.
Nobody ever swore at me — and there were
occasions when this was undoubtedly justified'

was a slow left-armer with a classical action who did not spin the ball enough, but he returned one summer to cause havoc in the County Championship as a medium-pace bowler with a bent arm who was able, on some wickets, to pitch leg and hit the off stump. He also had a lethal faster ball, which was quicker than most fast bowlers could produce, was a regular member of the England team and went on tour. Not surprisingly his great success bred many imitators.

Increasing numbers of pacemen discovered that they were able to gain a little extra pace or camouflage a slower ball with the aid of a jerk in their action. It has always seemed to me that Australia was more tolerant of bowlers with suspect actions than England, with our professional umpires. In the Thirties there were doubts about 'Dainty' Ironmonger and Eddie Gilbert, while post-war there were some who queried Geoff Noblett's bouncer, Charles Puckett, Ian Johnson and Jim Burke, but by the late Fifties the situation was somewhat out of control. It appeared to me that in 1958 every State team apart from

Queensland contained at least one bowler with a doubtful action, but with two of the MCC touring party probable pitchers, though not called, we could hardly complain.

The majority of the Australian offenders were what I termed 'throw draggers', with a method of delivery which was not dissimilar to that of a javelin thrower. Several years too late, the Australian administrators instigated an effective purge, while Tony Lock, having seen himself on slow-motion film, amended his action dramatically, successfully and bravely.

There was plenty of fun in the Fab Fifties, but there was also no shortage of fight.

Main picture: Edrich and Compton leave The Oval after England win a six-day Test to take the Ashes in 1953. Half a million people watched the series. From top: Jim Laker; Lancastrians Roy Tattersall and Brian Statham fly out to Australia in 1951; a Frank Tyson no-ball. Left: Laker and Lock at St Pancras in 1958 – next stop Tilbury, for Australia

The Sixties

THE TIMES THEY WERE A-CHANGING. SOMEONE HAD THE BRIGHT IDEA
OF STAGING A COUNTY GAME THAT WOULD BE OVER IN ONE DAY.
IT WAS THE START OF A ROLLER-COASTER RIDE THAT IS STILL GOING ON

BY
Henry Blofeld

the revolution of the Sixties was not confined to pop music and the lifestyle of the young. It was the decade in which English cricket also began to change. A process that seemed calmly controlled at first would spiral more violently in the succeeding decades.

English cricket in the 1960s still embraced the old order. Although professionals no longer emerged from different entrances at Lord's – that had stopped in 1946 – the initials of amateurs were still printed before their surnames on scorecards while those of the professionals came *after* their surnames and in the morning papers they were lucky if they got any at all. The principal domestic showpiece match was the Gentlemen against the Players at Lord's, but there were indications of approaching change in that five of the seventeen counties were already captained by professionals.

In 1962-3, the formal distinction between amateurs and professionals was abolished and inevitably the annual Gents v Players match was a casualty of that decision. Then, in 1963, the first knockout competition, the Gillette Cup, came into being as a result of the urgent need to try and find some way of bolstering county finances. The post-war boom years were over and gates had fallen disturbingly.

The introduction of limited-overs cricket was strongly opposed in some quarters because it was felt that the proceeds from a single day's cricket, especially if rain caused the game to spill over into a second or third day, would not be enough to make much of a difference. The solution was sponsorship. In 1963 the Gillette company underwrote the competition to the tune of £6,500, which now seems a most modest amount.

In that first year, the competition was called the First-Class Counties Knock-Out Competition for the Gillette Cup, before being abbreviated to the more manageable Gillette Cup. It made a very Heath Robinson sort of a start, too. To save expense, the players were billeted out in private houses, usually those of committee members, instead of being put up in hotels. That year the competition was also played over 65 overs an innings before being reduced to 60 in 1964 because too many matches had ended in bad light.

Since these tentative beginnings, limited-overs cricket

A Sixties landmark: Fred Trueman is congratulated by Colin Cowdrey on becoming the first bowler to take 300 Test wickets. Note the startling absence of high-fives from the rest of the England team

Main picture: West Indies'
Gary Sobers congratulates
new England captain Ray
Illingworth after a home
win at Headingley in 1959
to take the series 2-0.
Above: The Trueman drag
and the Sobers pirouette

has flourished both domestically and then, after the Packer revolution in the late Seventies, internationally as well. In England there are now three major domestic limited-overs competitions and the problem has been to keep a satisfactory balance between the one-day game and the traditional form of cricket.

The Sixties ended with the introduction of the John Player League, a 40-over competition between the first-class counties on Sunday afternoons – still the only league competition there has been. (It replaced the Sunday afternoon matches sponsored by Rothmans of Pall Mall in which The Cavaliers – a team made up of well-known players of the immediate past – took on county sides, with the not inconsiderable receipts usually going to the county's beneficiary of that year.)

Another significant step occurred in 1967 when overseas players were allowed to play for counties without a qualifying period of residence. This was part of an attempt to lift the quality and glamour of county cricket and so increase its popularity. Keith Boyce (Essex), John Shepherd (Kent) and Mushtaq Mohammad (Northampton-shire) were the first to sign, and they were soon joined by Mike Procter (Gloucestershire) and Barry Richards (Hampshire).

The last two came from South Africa, which at the end of this decade belatedly paid the penalty for its policies of apartheid, and its team was ostracised from international cricket. One effect of this was to flood the English market with South African cricketers who began digging up whatever English qualifications they could

Colin Cowdrey tosses up with Richie Benaud at Edgbaston to start the 1961 Ashes series, which Australia won 2-1. Top and left: A pair of English bulldogs – Ken Barrington and Colin Milburn. Kenny died in Barbados in 1981 while England's assistant manager. Ollie, a popular figure on TMS in the Eighties, died in 1990

'County cricket was becoming a more unrelenting profession and indeed, for some, a treadmill. Sundays off were a thing of the past – and that changed the character of the game'

West Indian all-rounder John Shepherd, of Kent. Right: Aussie opener Bill Lawry; Jim Parks appeals as Graeme Pollock is bowled by Freddie Titmus in 1965

find, in the hope of opening a back door into Test cricket. A few succeeded, while Kepler Wessels went on to play for Australia before apartheid was dismantled and South Africa rejoined the International Cricket Council.

The inevitable by-product of all these changes was beginning to appear by the end of the decade. Gradually, the limited-overs game and sponsorship increased the amount of money in cricket. The overseas players who came into county cricket were paid more than the home-grown cricketers – who were, not surprisingly, less than happy about it and wanted more themselves.

As the rewards for winning increased, so did the importance of victory and the need to bend the laws to the utmost to make sure of winning. The manners and morals of the game and its players began to decline as the ends were seen increasingly to justify the means. As a consequence, the pressure on the umpires started to increase. In defence of Sixties cricket, though, one must say that while the odd player was unshaven, designer stubble was to be a brainchild of the next two decades.

Tactically, the game also changed, again because of one-day cricket. The face of the bat was beginning to be opened by a generation of batsmen obsessed with the idea of running the ball down to third man for a single, undeterred by the presence of, at most, a slip and a gully. When attempted in Test cricket, where there can be as many as four slips and a gully, it is akin to suicide.

There was a growing preponderance of seam bowlers, dictated by the need to defend in limited-overs cricket. So, a generation of boring medium fast bowlers was born. Genuine pace bowlers, who are the strike bowlers of two-innings cricket, were discouraged because their lack of control could be expensive. The balance of the game was being decisively altered in that in one-day cricket it is better to restrict a side to 100 for no wicket in a 40-over innings than to bowl them out for 120. The best way to win a two-innings match is to bowl the opposition out twice. The traditional objectives were being stood on their head as a generation of defensive captains and bowlers came into being. The one plus point was that it greatly improved the standard of fielding.

1970s, when Packerism took a hand. It happened first in England because this was the only country trying to maintain a full professional system – which was becoming increasingly expensive at a time when leisure opportunities for the public had so greatly increased.

The changes begun in the Sixties were not all evident at the time. Colin Cowdrey remained the imponderably

West Indian sunshine at The Oval in 1963, where Conrad Hunte and Charlie Griffith gave Frank Worrell's team an eight-wicket victory. Far left: On tour in Australia – Eric rides pillion as the Bedser twins see the sights of Perth on a motor scooter. And a victorious arrival at Heathrow in 1968 for Tony Lock and Geoff Boycott – bat still in hand

With the advent of the Sunday League, county cricket was becoming a more unrelenting profession and indeed for some a treadmill. A first-class match would begin on the Saturday; one or even both sides might have to travel a hundred miles or more for their Sunday League match and then back again on Sunday evening to continue the first-class match on the Monday. Sundays off were a thing of the past – and that changed the character of county cricket, just as the disappearance of the rest day in Test cricket has sadly altered the character of Test matches.

While the character of English cricket began to change, cricket overseas was not so affected until the late

elegant strokemaker he had always been. Gary Sobers was as flourishingly impetuous, Bill Lawry as defiant and obstinate; Hanif Mohammad as precise and compact; Ray Illingworth just as Yorkshire and curmudgeonly.

The winds of change had begun to blow nonetheless, and by the end of the decade they were beginning to ruffle shirts and flick the Beatle-length hair that poked increasingly out from the back of caps. In the Seventies, close fielders would speak less endearingly to batsmen, the pressure on umpires would increase, and on a hot day coats (though not ties) could be removed in the Pavilion at Lord's. The Sixties have a lot to answer for.

The Seventies

IN A DECADE OF MANY, MANY GREAT NAMES – LILLEE, HOLDING, BOTHAM, GAVASKAR – THE MAN WHO DOMINATED CRICKET DIDN'T BOWL, BAT OR FIELD. BUT KERRY PACKER CERTAINLY PLAYED TO WIN

BY Christopher Martin-Jenkins

A bad moon rising? The arrival of World Series Cricket, with its floodlights, pyjamas and dolly birds, left the cricket establishment in the dark. In 1977 Australian tycoon Kerry Packer took on the Test and County Cricket Board in the Law Courts – and came out smiling

The 1970s came in like a lamb and went out like a lion. The decade began with much brilliant cricket from half a dozen or more great players; it saw the emergence of several of the fiercest fast bowlers of all time; it marked the outlawing of South Africa at the very moment that they were dominating Test cricket for the first time; and it will always be notorious for the greatest upheaval in the game's long history. Cricket at professional level changed for ever in 1977.

On 8 May, two months after a wonderfully successful match at Melbourne to mark the Centenary of the first Test between Australia and England, the story broke that most of the best players in the world were involved in a clandestine revolution.

The man who was planning to overthrow cricket's Old Guard was a television mogul from Sydney, Australia. Kerry Packer's father, Frank, had built a powerful media business. His commercially fearless offspring set out to expand it with a ruthlessness no one had anticipated. Cricket was booming in the mid-1970s, especially in Australia, where Dennis Lillee and Jeff Thomson had proved too fast for England in 1974-5 and for Clive

Lloyd's West Indian team a year later. Kerry Packer wanted the Australian television rights and he was prepared to pay whatever it took to get them.

The sum turned out to be far greater than he had imagined. The Australian Cricket Board, happy that the Australian Broadcasting Commission had served cricket faithfully through good and bad times, was not prepared for the new kid on the block to muscle in and buy the exclusive rights he had demanded when the ABC's contract expired. Packer's reaction was to buy up 18 Australians and 17 of the finest players from the rest of the world to play a series of one-, three- and five-day matches, for prize money of $100,000 in addition to individual salaries far in excess of anything they had previously been paid.

Perceiving the threat to the established order, the International Cricket Council first tried to compromise, then went to the High Court and lost. It invited Mr Packer to Lord's in June. By now 51 players had signed to play in the rebel circus. The ICC actually offered to accept a series of matches, provided that they lasted no more than six weeks and did not interrupt its own

A modest stage for two mighty stars: Gordon Greenidge and Barry Richards, arguably the greatest openers of their era, turn out for Hampshire. Right: Dennis Lillee in full flow at Trent Bridge, 1973, as Tony Greig backs up

programme. Packer was also offered the chance to bid for the Australian TV rights to Test matches when the ABC contract expired, in 1981, but without guaranteed exclusivity. Packer, holding the real aces – the players – angrily rejected the deal, telling the media outside the pavilion: 'Now it's every man for himself and the Devil take the hindmost.'

It was a struggle to get a microphone close enough to this suddenly famous man during perhaps the most emotive press conference I have ever attended. The

Australian tycoon was holding world cricket to ransom.

At the subsequent court case, wherein his case was put with sparkling expertise by Robert Alexander, later chairman of NatWest Bank, much was made of the ease with which he had lured away underpaid international players. In fact, Greg Chappell had just written a book entitled *The 100th Summer* in which he observed that 'cricketers' rewards have increased dramatically in a comparatively short time… Cash endorsements are flowing as never before and the (Australian) Test team is sponsored now for three years.'

Having established his right to employ the players and to use several of the established cricket grounds, Packer and his associates embarked on two expensive seasons' play during which they introduced floodlit night cricket – soon to prove a brilliantly successful concept for hot countries – coloured clothing and aggressive marketing. When peace was made between his companies and the Australian Cricket Board, his reward was a long-term contract to televise official international cricket and another to market the game in Australia.

The cover of the 1971 *Wisden* had given clues to the tumult which lay only a few years ahead. Three of the highlighted topics within were: The South African Tour Dispute; England v. The Rest of the World; Thrills of Sunday Cricket. Discontented South African cricketers gave Mr Packer a rich source of talent when he and his accomplices, who included the England captain Tony Greig and the former Australian captain Richie Benaud, began to plan their coup, based on a Rest of the World side; and 'Sunday thrills', transferred to the international arena, gave him one of the marketing tools he needed.

The only disappointed players when the 'World Series' matches finished were the South Africans, to whom the matches had offered the unique buzz of international cricket which they had not enjoyed since their government's apartheid policies finally led to their isolation in 1970. From a cricketing angle, that was sad: they had thrashed Australia at home in all four matches of their 1969-70 series, with two majestic batsmen in Barry Richards and Graeme Pollock, a superb all-rounder, Mike Procter, and other high-class cricketers in Eddie Barlow,

Tuning in to the future: Kerry Packer listens to microphones under the pitch on the first day of World Series Cricket at Melbourne in 1977. Above left: Bank teller Tina Jepps helps Graeme Pollock to carry the 75,000 South African rand (£50,000) which persuaded him to sign up with Packer. Left: If Lillee don't get you, Thommo will

Pace bowlers dominated the decade, but India relied on their spinners, including left-armer Bishan Bedi (rarely seen without his turban) and leg spinner Chandrasekhar. Right: India's batting genius Sunil Gavaskar and Australia's hard-hitting wicketkeeper Rod Marsh

Peter Pollock, Trevor Goddard and Denis Lindsay.

The decade that ended so dramatically for Australia, in fact, was not one of their more distinguished. They were beaten at home by Ray Illingworth's England team in 1970-1 and again, with a Packer-weakened side, by Mike Brearley's side of 1978-9. In the intervening series, with the emergence of a thoroughbred fast bowler in Dennis Lillee, the discovery of the immensely strong and dangerously fast Jeff Thomson, and the support of the tough and classy Chappell brothers, plus Rodney Marsh, Doug Walters, Ashley Mallett and Max Walker, they swept aside England and the West Indies in successive home series. Yet in England in 1977, missing only Ian Chappell and Lillee, they won no Tests and just five of their 22 first-class matches, such was the effect on

morale of the secret assignations to World Series Cricket.

While the Ashes were changing hands so rapidly, India were winning in England for the first time with a trio of marvellous spin bowlers in Bedi, Venkataraghavan and Chandrasekhar and a batsman of perfect technique and almost perfect temperament, Sunil Gavaskar; and Pakistan were showing they could be a force anywhere by declaring on 608 for seven at Edgbaston in 1971, with 274 by Zaheer Abbas and centuries from Mushtaq Mohammad and Asif Iqbal. That same team included Imran Khan, Majid Khan, Wasim Bari and Intikhab Alam, every one of them a player of rare talent.

What a decade it was! England had John Snow, Alan Knott and Colin Cowdrey in 1970, and Ian Botham, David Gower and Graham Gooch by 1978. Gary Sobers was still playing Test cricket until 1974; so were Lance Gibbs and Rohan Kanhai. Gordon Greenidge, Viv Richards, and the pace quartet of Michael Holding, Joel

'The pace quartet of Michael Holding, Joel Garner, Andy Roberts and Colin Crioft had all emerged under Clive Lloyd's captaincy – and World Series Cricket had given them a licence to unleash the ball at the head and body'

Garner, Andy Roberts and Colin Croft had all emerged under Clive Lloyd's captaincy within a few years.

World Series Cricket had given them a licence to unleash the ball at the head and body, and it was this – and the growing realisation of the attraction of one-day night cricket – which changed the game for good … or bad.

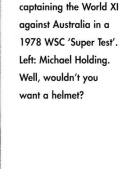

Tony Greig puts on his batting helmet for one of his last appearances, captaining the World XI against Australia in a 1978 WSC 'Super Test'. Left: Michael Holding. Well, wouldn't you want a helmet?

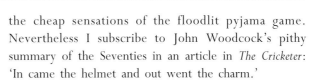

Test cricket has so far survived, quite triumphantly, the assault from the one-day international which had its genesis in the turbulent Seventies. Shane Warne and the leg-spin revival has been a kind of counter-revolution to the cheap sensations of the floodlit pyjama game. Nevertheless I subscribe to John Woodcock's pithy summary of the Seventies in an article in *The Cricketer*: 'In came the helmet and out went the charm.'

The Eighties

ENGLAND WERE A TEAM OF SUPERSTARS. BOTHAM, GOWER, GATTING, GOOCH AND WILLIS TOOK TURNS AT BEING CAPTAIN. BUT, HEADINGLEY '81 EXCEPTED, SOMEHOW THE RESULTS JUST WENT FROM BAD TO WORSE

BY

Vic Marks

Circket, lovely cricket ... the familiar sound of willow on leather – and wood on bone when the inevitable pitch invasion occurs. Opposite: Umpire Mervyn Kitchen tries vainly to save his stumps at Trent Bridge after Pakistan reach the 1983 World Cup semi-finals. Inset: Joel Garner and Viv Richards – two of the players who made West Indies kings of the decade

*i*n 1980 international cricket tiptoed hesitantly back to normality after the stunning intervention of Mr Kerry Packer. Despite all the bitterness that his audacious scheme had engendered, despite the fact that he was spectacularly successful in achieving his aims – those TV rights (he was curiously reticent about supplanting TMS) – the transition was remarkably swift and smooth.

Packer's intrusion into the world of cricket was not all bad. The introduction of night cricket in Australia created a magnificent spectacle, even if the first English tourists to play under floodlights were initially sceptical. The lights were dazzling and those coloured pyjamas were jolly undignified, yet the pylons in Sydney and later Melbourne and Perth transformed the grounds into vibrant amphitheatres that quickly seduced the Australian public and inevitably aroused the adrenalin of the most laid-back cricketer. Soon everyone agreed that night cricket was an adornment to the game, even if the proliferation of one-day matches wasn't.

Tony Greig, Packer's most enthusiastic henchman, repeatedly claimed that cricketers were better paid post-

Packer. Perhaps they were at international level. In England, Cornhill continued to sponsor Test cricket, and it was possible for a regular Test cricketer to become a relatively wealthy man. Soon England's finest could be spotted entering the dressing room clutching briefcases and portable phones; many acquired agents and wine cellars.

Packer had insisted that his cricket should be 'macho' and thereby hastened two trends which baffled cricketers of an earlier generation – the advent of helmets and a new preoccupation with physical fitness.

At the beginning of the decade, county professionals were unable to stifle their giggles as Dennis Amiss strode out to bat at Edgbaston looking like an ageing Hell's Angel with his white motorbike helmet perched on top of his head. Yet within a year or two only a fool or a genius eschewed the helmet. Throughout the Eighties only Viv Richards declined to wear one, just in case he gave the impression that the bowler had a chance. Initially there was an unseemly scrabble in dressing rooms to grab the team helmet, especially when playing against West Indian pacemen. Soon, cagey county pros

'At the beginning of the decade,
county professionals were unable to stifle their giggles
as Dennis Amiss strode out to bat at Edgbaston
looking like an ageing Hell's Angel with his
white motorbike helmet perched on top of his head.
Yet within a year or two only a fool or a genius
eschewed the helmet'

Far left: Gary Sobers looks askance as Dennis Amiss practises in the nets in his white helmet. But the famous incident in which Mike Gatting had his nose rearranged by a Malcolm Marshall bouncer in 1986 proved the helmet's worth, particularly when facing the West Indies

made sure that they had acquired one of their own and they checked that they had packed their helmet first, their bat second.

Cricketers began to spend a lot of time in tracksuits – Packer had insisted that each of his teams should have a full-time physio. Now most sides indulged in a range of exotic stretching exercises. At 9.45 every morning, the time when I imagine Denis Compton was abusing his alarm clock and contemplating how to get to the ground (which ground?), most cricketers were locked in a ham-string stretch. Graham Gooch in particular applauded this development, rather more enthusiastically than England's captain at the start of the decade, Ian Botham.

Perhaps the most important consequence of the Packer Affair was that it revealed to the top players that they were saleable commodities, with a definite value in the marketplace. It did not take long for those ostracised in South Africa to realise that if there were enough noughts on the cheque, it was possible to tempt players away from traditional cricket. Gooch led the first rebel

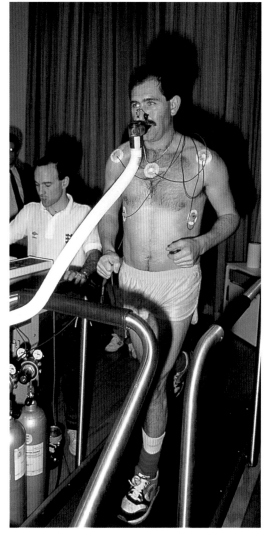

To train or not to train, that was the question. A succession of England captains had distinctly differing views. Graham Gooch was a believer. Ian Botham and David Gower weren't so sure

tour in 1982 and several more followed before the transformation in South Africa.

The authorities also became more commercially minded. No new stand was constructed without corridors of suave boxes complete with the essentials of corporate hospitality – a bar, a television, and an invitation to Henry Blofeld to address them at lunchtime.

Defections to South Africa hastened the decline of England and Australia in world cricket, which was dominated by the West Indies throughout the decade. The pacemen ruled and the West Indies stuck rigidly to an attack of four fast bowlers under the leadership of Clive Lloyd and Viv Richards, who acted as foremen of an unrelenting rota system that seldom failed. Pakistan, India and New Zealand, blessed with their great all-rounders Imran Khan, Kapil Dev and Richard Hadlee, could no longer be taken for granted, though it was still a stunning achievement for India to win the World Cup in 1983. There were times when England and Australia seemed to be playing not only for the Ashes but also the wooden spoon of international cricket, though Australia did eventually recover their self-esteem under the dogged leadership of Allan Border. But it didn't matter. An Ashes series retained its glamour.

For England the decade swung from ecstasy to agony. The excitement of the summer of 1981 has seldom been surpassed, provided you are a Pom. Botham went from villain to hero within a fortnight. Brearley was recalled, Marsh and Lillee were crestfallen to win a 500/1 bet. Where were you when Botham went berserk at

Headingley? I would have loved to have been there (in fact I had the rather less uplifting task of bowling David Steele to a hundred at Taunton) – and at Edgbaston and Old Trafford.

But there was no pleasure for Englishmen at Headingley in 1989. Amid much ballyhoo and some subterfuge the new chairman of selectors, Ted Dexter, had recalled David Gower as captain. In the first match at Leeds Gower inserted the Aussies, who scored 601 for seven declared, winning by 210 runs. Thereafter England subsided. They used 29 players that summer to the Aussies' 12; half the team opted to rebel in South Africa and they lost the series 4-0.

Fortunately, Lord Ted was 'not aware of making any mistakes'. Well, he did pick a frail, angelic-looking 21-year-old Mancunian for the final two Tests of the series. His name was Michael Atherton and we all wondered whether he was any good – but that is one of the stories of the Nineties…

It may not be the village green, but there are few more inspiring sights in sport than the Sydney Cricket Ground by night

The Nineties

AN EMOTIONAL RETURN FOR SOUTH AFRICA. A STUNNING WORLD CUP
WIN FOR SRI LANKA. A DECADE OF SURPRISES – BUT THE BIGGEST
OF ALL IS THAT THE WORLD'S MOST FEARED BOWLER IS A LEG SPINNER

BY
**Chris
Cowdrey**

it has been the nervous Nineties for England as the battle for world Test supremacy continues. There have been intermittent claims from West Indies, Pakistan and South Africa, yet Australia has been the dominant force.

1990 saw the start of major change within cricket. The ICC under the chairmanship of Sir Colin Cowdrey introduced a code of conduct to try to stem the tide of declining over rates, endless short-pitched bowling and incessant 'sledging'. Only now are we beginning to see the benefits of such a timely intervention.

In the short term the code may have contributed to the downfall of West Indies' supremacy, as the four-pronged pace attack battled to achieve 15 overs per hour, fines ensued and the bouncer was restricted. Gradually the spinner is featuring more in Test cricket and the wrist spinner has re-emerged as a vital attacking weapon. In the 1990s every Test-playing country has selected a leg spinner or a left arm unorthodox bowler (Australia Shane Warne, England Ian Salisbury, India Anil Kumble, New Zealand Greg Loveridge, Pakistan Mushtaq Ahmed, South Africa Paul Adams, Sri Lanka

Asoka de Silva, West Indies Shivnarine Chanderpaul and Zimbabwe Paul Strang).

The ICC's most radical step was to bring in a referee for all international matches to oversee the new code of conduct. Can they have imagined that this move could have such ramifications? The early Nineties were marred by the dreaded ball-tampering saga, which brought the match referee into direct confrontation with players and dragged the game of cricket into the High Court.

The suspicion that the Pakistan team were engaging in ball-tampering over and above the age-old practice of 'picking the seam' was brought to a head when England's Allan Lamb accused them publicly. The allegations appeared to be borne out by television footage in court. A year later Michael Atherton was caught red-handed with earth in his pocket which was supposedly being applied to the ball, and following furious debate and an apology from the England captain, the whole incident was dismissed in a shroud of mystery.

What it did unearth was the whole aspect of 'reverse swing'. For years it had been talked about, and there were many theories as to why a ball should suddenly

Opposite: Signs of the times. It was sometimes hard to tell cricket supporters from soccer fans as the Barmy Army followed England round the globe. Cricketers' dress styles changed, too, with the adoption of designer sunglasses – modelled here by Graham Gooch, former England manager Raymond Illingworth, and Australia's sunshine superstar Shane Warne

Allan Lamb (top) and Ian Botham suffered a reverse swing when they took Imran Khan to court in 1996, claiming he had called them racists and Botham a cheat. Imran said he was misquoted. Darren Gough, England's breath of fresh air, led the charge to acquire the Pakistani art of reverse swing with an old ball

swing the opposite way to that expected by the likes of Bedser, Sobers and Trueman. Is it only as a result of subterfuge, or has there been a development in technology or technique? Is it only possible if delivered by a genuinely fast bowler? Is it really true that bottle tops were being used to deface the ball and the holes in the ball filled up with earth to weigh one side down?

Soon there were many purveyors of the new bowling skill. The king of reverse swing was Waqar Younis, but suddenly Darren Gough learned the art, and he too can produce the late in-swinging yorker with an old ball. There is no suggestion that Gough might be cheating, which anyway is impossible now that the umpires have been instructed to inspect the ball on a regular basis. It has been a busy time for match referees and umpires, and as a result of their close attention, tampering with the ball seems to have ceased.

Another new role in the Nineties is the neutral, or should I say independent, umpire. The traditional two 'home' umpires had become a serious bone of contention, but bringing in overseas umpires was resisted on financial grounds. The solution lay in sponsorship by National Grid. The presence of an outsider in every match has brought greater respect for umpires, and the standard of umpiring is improving all the time.

There is enormous pressure on umpires these days, due to the intense scrutiny of television replays and today's more opinionated commentator. This has been alleviated by the ICC's introduction of the third umpire, who sits in the stand and adjudicates on stumpings and run-outs while everyone waits anxiously for the red or green light. Gone are the days of 'if in doubt, not out'.

One area of little doubt is that the limited-overs game continues to prosper, and the crowds flock to see the day/night floodlit matches. Although English fans are unlikely to experience this great spectacle for climatic reasons, elsewhere we may soon see Test cricket under lights becoming the rage. We have witnessed coloured clothing at Lords in the Nineties, but surely never floodlights. It is hard to imagine batsmen walking out to their own theme song at the home of cricket, but there is increasing pressure to compete with this more marketable product from the southern hemisphere, and I suspect there are other gimmicks just round the corner.

For those who felt that the one-day international was becoming too predictable, Sri Lanka's triumph in the 1995 World Cup proved yet again that in sport you should always expect the unexpected. They were a delight to watch, playing with gay abandon — and had a point to prove: that they should by now be playing a full

Test series in England. Winning a limited-overs trophy, albeit the World Cup, does not give them the right to cut corners into a congested programme, yet we would all love to see more of Sri Lanka.

As surprising was England's 3-0 defeat in Zimbabwe in a one-day series in 1997. The Zimbabweans did not disgrace themselves in the two Test Matches, either, and the inaugural fixture in Bulawayo ended with the scores level, match drawn.

Down the road from the relative tranquillity of Zimbabwe we witnessed the greatest single event of the Nineties. Following the release of Nelson Mandela in 1990, South Africa were re-admitted to the international arena after 29 years in the wilderness. They first headed for India, which was not only politically correct but prudent considering the huge trade between the two countries. The South Africans eventually returned to Lord's in 1994 with a resounding victory, which was a memorable and moving affair. Welcome back, I say.

It is Australia, however, who have enjoyed most prosperity as a cricketing nation. Throughout the decade they have been the major force and just as their pace attack began to look frail, Shane Warne appeared on the

The age of accusations. Pakistan's deadly duo of Wasim Akram and Waqar Younis rose above claims of doctoring the ball, but England captain Michael Atherton was caught on camera putting dirt on the ball during the 1995 Lord's Test against South Africa

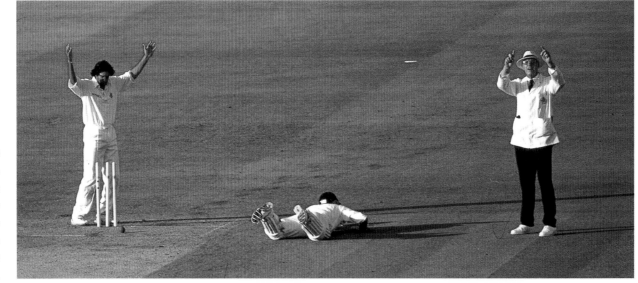

Typical scenes from the age of the electronic eye. The umpire signals for a TV replay. The players cluster in an anxious mob. The third umpire scans the replay. The traffic light turns red. Then a giant hand comes out of the pavilion and pushes the batsman off. (Actually we made that last bit up.)

'There is huge pressure on umpires these days, due to the intense scrutiny of TV replays. This has led to the introduction of the third umpire, who adjudicates on run-outs while everyone waits anxiously for the red or green light. Gone are the days of 'if in doubt, not out'.

scene. With 240 wickets from 52 Tests he is sure to break all records, and has set the example for all leg spinners to follow.

The much-acclaimed Australian 'Academy' produced Warne and a host of other fine young cricketers, and it would be foolish for other nations not to learn from their infrastructure. They also the innate advantage of a

does not really qualify, and the same goes for the bowling of Steve Waugh – though the gritty New South Wales man has arguably been Brian Lara's main rival as the decade's leading batsman).

Perhaps the most dramatic change within cricket has been the advance in physical fitness to a level on a par with most other sports. This has produced a remarkably

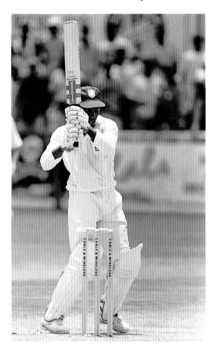

The world's top batsman, the world's top bowler – and the world's top appealer. Brian Lara of the West Indies broke Gary Sobers' world record with his innings of 375 against England in 1993-4; Shane Warne has taken 240 Test wickets in the Nineties; and England's irrepressible Dominic Cork has also made his presence felt

climate conducive to hard pitches and an outdoor way of life which produces a more naturally fit animal. Aligned to an aggressive approach, pride in performance and above all pride in the 'green and gold' of Australia, you have a formidable beast.

In 1997 the England and Wales Cricket Board has been formed under the chairmanship of Lord MacLaurin, the chairman of Tesco. He is charged with the task of re-establishing English cricket on a sound footing and producing a national team to compete with the old enemy.

One mystery of the Nineties has been the disappearance of the world-class all-rounder. After the likes of Sir Richard Hadlee, Kapil Dev, Ian Botham and Imran Khan in the Eighties, this decade can only offer Brian McMillan of South Africa (Wasim Akram's batting

high standard of outfielding, but it also brings an ever-increasing injury toll.

The greatest loss to cricket and the TEST MATCH SPECIAL commentary box was the death of Brian Johnston in 1994. I am sure Johnners would have been happy to see that the game is set fair for the Millennium, though he would have longed for a transformation in England's fortunes. He would have loved to see the leg spinners wheeling away, and have enjoyed the thrill of the 1997 Ashes series.

Of course, he might have frowned upon some things – well, we are all a bit sensitive when something rather too radical or progressive threatens the game of cricket. But all too often we just shrug our shoulders and say: 'We're in the Nineties now, you know.'

Champagne Moments

LISTENERS AND COMMENTATORS RECALL THEIR FAVOURITE INCIDENTS FROM 40 YEARS OF TEST MATCH SPECIAL

My serious interest in cricket coincided with the beginning of John Arlott's commentaries at the end of the war. As a young boy brought up on Beeb voices like Alvar Liddell and John Snagge, it was riveting to hear a man with an accent like the farmer down the lane describing the alluring mysteries of the first-class cricket field – the long legs, the maidens, the short fine legs, and all those slips!

I won't choose as my Champagne Moment his last commentary; that was too sad. So here is one of his little gems.

The Lord's Test, England v Pakistan, I think 1960. On Saturday morning the England fielding had been atrocious. Three or four catches dropped ... at least. John came on immediately after lunch – not his favourite session. 'So, it's Trueman to bowl from the nursery end and the field is mustered.' A theatrical pause – and then, vehemently – 'E-R-E-D, not A-R-D!!'
– *John W. A. Thurstans, Penzance*

TEST MATCH SPECIAL
Quiz
• THE SIXTIES •

3 Who was the last bowler to dismiss Peter May in Test cricket?

Answer on page 120

FRED TRUEMAN'S CHAMPAGNE MOMENT

The day I joined the team

When TEST MATCH SPECIAL was born in 1957, I was still playing – taking on the West Indies. When I looked up at the commentary box, I never thought that one day I would be part of that most important programme.

So it was a very special moment when I joined John Arlott, the voice of cricket, and that wonderful man Brian Johnston, the practical joker who was a great broadcaster but at heart was a boy who never grew up. I don't think we shall ever see the like of Arlott and Johnston again.

Any young men who follow in the footsteps of Trevor Bailey or myself will be very fortunate if they have the same happiness that we have had.

MIKE SELVEY'S CHAMPAGNE MOMENT

A Sri Lankan wake-up call

Arjuna Ranatunga angling the ball to third man to complete Sri Lanka's victory over Australia in the 1996 World Cup final. It served, I hope, as a boot up the backside of anyone connected with cricket in this country.

My Champagne Moment was hearing that 'hard man' of cricket Sir Richard Hadlee in the TEST MATCH SPECIAL commentary box. Was he talking about his fast bowling technique? No. He was doing an impression of Basil Brush!
– *Helen Crossland, Huddersfield*

The best times are when rain stops play! I recall years ago on a rainy stint at Headingley the TEST MATCH SPECIAL team all getting involved in a heated discussion about ... what types of trees were planted in a row behind the ground at the Kirkstall Lane End. (I think the conclusion they eventually came to was Cornish elms.)

But I also treasure the countless occasions when, despite the continued commentary from the 'front' of the box, you just knew that the rest of the TMS team were convulsed in stifled giggling behind their microphones.
– *Alexandra D. C. Ross, Harrogate*

· THE COMMENTATORS' CHOICE ·
Shane Warne's first ball in England

Chosen by Vic Marks, Neville Oliver and Trevor Bailey, who pithily describes it thus:
'The ball from Shane Warne from over the wicket at Old Trafford which pitched just outside Mike Gatting's
leg stump and hit his off stump and quite understandably caused mayhem in the England side'

PATRICK MOORE:
I am an avid 'watcher' of TMS. I think I best remember that magic moment when we were at grips with Australia at The Oval in 1968, Derek Underwood was at his best and only John Inverarity was keeping England at bay. The ball when Derek finally netted John Inverarity to win the match was a great moment indeed.
And of course nothing can ever beat Brian Johnston's 'There's Harvey, standing with his legs apart, waiting for a tickle...'

● *Patrick Moore's The Sky at Night this year celebrated its own 40th anniversary*

NEVILLE OLIVER:

The First Test of the 1993 Ashes series gave us the Champagne Moment to out-bubble all others.

Australia batted first and were all out for 289. In reply, Gooch and Atherton pushed England's score to 71 before the first wicket fell. In the TMS box the main topic of conversation was the absence of Shane Warne from the bowling crease. Body language almost suggested Australian captain Allan Border was grumpy with Warne and was ignoring him. Perhaps it was to raise anticipation.

But as Mike Gatting started his innings, Border called up the 23-year-old leg spinner. A roar of appreciation went up from the Old Trafford crowd. Johnners said: 'About time.'

Warne measured out his run and spent a little time discussing field placings with his captain. The crowd hushed as he came in. Aggers moved to the edge of his chair to describe the approach of the leg spinner.

JONATHAN AGNEW: *'Now there must be a little bit of pressure on young Warne's shoulders, I would think, here. Because he'll know that his team are expecting him to come on and take some wickets, or at least turn the ball.*

'And here comes Shane Warne off only two or three paces. He bowls and Gatting is taken on the pad ... he's bowled!

'Well, Gatting's still standing there. He can't believe it, but that must have turned a very long way.

VIC MARKS:
4 June 1993, Old Trafford. Shane Warne's first delivery in Test cricket in England. It set off on the line of Mike Gatting's pads and then dipped in the air further towards the leg side until it was 18 inches adrift of the stumps. By this time Gatting was beginning to lose interest ... until the ball bounced, turned and fizzed across his ample frame to clip the off bail. This moment heralded the arrival of Warne and the demise of England in the 1993 series, but also ushered in an exciting era in which the ball no longer had to be propelled at 90mph to terrify Test batsmen.

It took his off stump. Gatting can't believe it.

'That is Shane Warne's first delivery in a Test Match in England. He's comprehensively bowled Mike Gatting. That must have turned an awful long way.'

TREVOR BAILEY: *'Well, that's the Champagne Moment.'*

It was as though time had stopped still. For a millisecond there was utter silence. Then the crowd erupted with a roar that defies description. Warne and the Australians celebrated a wicket like never before or since. Poor Mike Gatting could not understand how he was out.

In the TMS box Johnners roared his approval and all I could do was laugh. That night in the Cornhill tent Mike Gatting, in the manner of the bloody good bloke that he is, said: 'In 20 years that ball will have pitched five feet outside leg to hit off.'

Probably right. Good stories always get substantial embellishment and this one deserves it. Champagne Moments will never be the same.

TEST MATCH SPECIAL
Quiz
· THE SIXTIES ·

4 Who captained South Africa on their last tour of England before 1994?

Answer on page 120

Where cricket meets Alice in Wonderland

DAVID CAVANAGH VISITS 'AN OASIS OF FAIR PLAY, WONDERFUL LANGUAGE AND SURREAL HUMOUR' – THE TMS COMMENTARY BOX AT TRENT BRIDGE. THE ONLY PROBLEM IS SQUEEZING IN

It's approaching lunchtime on Friday, 5 July 1996 and there is a capacity crowd in the Larwood & Voce Tavern at Trent Bridge. To order a drink, you have to lean precariously over a perimeter fence of sweaty, salmon-red male torsos at the bar. It is one of the hottest days of the year.

Today is the second day of the Third Test between England and India. A television set on the wall is replaying the dismissal (for nought) of Anil Kumble. As he walks back to the pavilion, several patrons of the Larwood & Voce offer taunting ululations, raising their middle fingers to the screen. It's not a particularly pleasant atmosphere; sizing these lads up is an undertaking best approached clandestinely.

Not far away, however, lies a little oasis of fair play, wonderful language and surreal humour – sadly, one of the last such oases in the modern-day desert of broadcasting. It is reached by ascending the steep white stairs of the members' pavilion, edging past the lunchtime food trays stacked up in a narrow corridor, and taking a right turn into the TEST MATCH SPECIAL commentary box.

To spend the Friday of the Trent Bridge Test in the TMS box is a delightful idea in theory, but it's an awkward business in practice. Of three rooms giving on to the ground, the TMS team has managed to commandeer the one that directly overlooks the wicket (Richie Benaud's BBC1 unit and Ian Botham's Sky boys are ensconced in rooms to either side), but this vantage point comes at a price: it is little bigger than a child's bedroom.

Indeed, it's the pokiest box on the Test circuit. This is stated in a resigned voice by Jonathan Agnew, the friendly, house captain-like Cricket Correspondent for the BBC. Agnew, having just finished a 20-minute stint of commentary, has popped out to the corridor for a breather. As his chair is now occupied by Henry Blofeld, there is no room for Agnew in the commentary box. At his feet he spies a pile of plastic trays, each containing a compartmentalised cold-meat salad. This will be lunch. 'Dan-Air, Malaga,' he mutters grimly.

The TEST MATCH SPECIAL team's proud claim is that it can send commentary from anywhere under any circumstances. Agnew recalls a crowd riot at Jamshedpur

Standing room only. The duo immortalised by the legendary 'Legover Incident' – Aggers and Johnners – snuggle up with The Bearded Wonder in their natural habitat, the commentary box at The Oval

Peter Baxter, stopwatch in hand, and his assistant Shilpa Patel eye Jonathan Agnew's mouthwatering 'Dan Air Malaga' airplane lunch

in India; when the rioters ran out of rocks, they tore the 2's, 3's and 4's off the scoreboard and started throwing them like frisbees. Agnew's own journey to the Jamshedpur ground had taken ten hours by bus, during which he had been held up by bandits.

'It's hard sometimes when you're on the sixth day of a fourteen-week tour and you phone home and the wife's in tears,' he admits. 'It isn't always the riotous fun that people imagine. A lot of it's very lonely. I can remember a great thrill running through me in a Rawalpindi hotel room one afternoon when I managed to locate *Scooby Doo* on the Cartoon Channel.'

Here at Trent Bridge, in the commentary box to which Agnew has now returned, six people have squeezed themselves into seated or standing positions. (The door is held ajar by a large basket of fruit.) On the far left, facing the window, sits Chris Cowdrey, the former Kent and England captain. This Test is Cowdrey's debut as a TMS summariser. It's easy to see that he will be an extremely good one: he has brought with him a keen knowledge of player psychology, which he relays to the listeners laconically and insightfully. All Cowdrey needs in order to become a fully paid-up member of the TMS team is a nickname.

Agnew, who was long ago re-christened Aggers by the late Brian Johnston, sits in the middle in the commentator's chair, doing the lion's share of the talking. While he and Cowdrey trade air-time, although none of the listeners can see them, they nevertheless turn to look at one another as though they were having a conversation in a pub or in a park. When a wicket falls, they both lean back in their chairs.

To Agnew's right sits Bill Frindall, alias The Bearded Wonder. A small-ish, scholarly-looking character with his spectacles on a chain, Frindall's role as the scorer permits him to be an occasional interruptor. A TMS perennial since 1965, he is the programme's longest-serving member. Nowadays he has a computer by his side.

On a chair to the rear of the room sits Shilpa, the assistant to the producer, Peter Baxter. (Shilpa is believed to be the only woman to be allowed in the members' pavilion during the Lord's Test Match.) Baxter himself,

a man with the demeanour of a benevolent headmaster, stands in the middle of the room, monitoring the proceedings with a stop-watch. It is his job – among others – to compose the day's duty roster, to check on the whereabouts of the persistently late Christopher Martin-Jenkins, and to wield the sword of power if necessary. He mentions a Test at Georgetown, Guyana, in 1990, where torrential rain wiped out all five days' play. On the second day, none of his commentary team even bothered turning up at the ground. Baxter, finding them in the hotel bar, threatened to withhold their fees for non-attendance. On the third completely washed-out day, the entire commentary team reported promptly for duty.

Finally, seated next to Shilpa is Graeme Fowler, the former opening batsman whose excellent summaries at one-day level have won him an upgrade to Test status. He has replaced the equally Lancastrian David 'Bumble' Lloyd. At this moment Fowler is waiting for Baxter – TMS's producer since 1973 – to give him the nod to replace Cowdrey in the summariser's chair. Once on air he can have bizarre, pedantic discussions with Agnew such as:

Agnew: 'What's the difference, then, between a noodle and a nurdle?'

Fowler: 'A nurdle is more stolid, I suppose.'

In the post-lunch lull, some Trent Bridge claret is uncorked. There is a mood of relaxed, confident broadcasting. Everyone is given 20 minutes on-air at a time, at which point there is a speedy changeover. When Agnew vacates his chair to allow the next incumbent to begin commentating, the following exchange takes place:

'Blowers.'

'My dear old thing.'

The new arrival, sporting a cravat and glasses, resembles a cross between Anton Rodgers in *Fresh Fields* and a character out of *Alice In Wonderland*. This is Henry 'Blowers' Blofeld, the owner of one of England's fruitiest voices. This morning he received a letter from a Mrs Joan Jones in Shipley which read in part: 'I just have to write to tell you what a fabulous voice you have, a voice I could listen to all day.'

It would be hard to disagree with Mrs Jones. Blofeld is an individual whose old-world cordiality and cultured vocabulary mark him out as little short of a national treasure in an age of sport-bites, clichés and Americanisms. Nobody will ever hear Blofeld utter the now-ubiquitous words 'ahead of' to indicate 'in preparation for'. He looks as if he wouldn't even know how to programme a video.

'I went off to Sky,' he informs us languidly of his brief absence from TMS in the early 1990s. 'They made me an offer my bank manager couldn't refuse. But they wanted me to scream and shout and do all this frightful nonsense, so back I came.'

It is no surprise that Sky's style proved too much for the fastidious Blowers. The 36-year-old Agnew, who is a good 20 years Blofeld's junior, views the man fondly. 'He is, I suppose, the English eccentric,' says Agnew. 'He's got this thing about pigeons and buses. That's Blowers.'

Blofeld's on-air excursions – searching for the correct collective noun for a group of starlings – are very enjoyable. But Blofeld is cricket through-and-through. An excellent batsman in his youth, he was earmarked as an England opener of the future, until injury ended his playing career. He seems to enjoy the crowds that cricket attracts, finding the best in everyone and reporting to TMS listeners the latest antics of the spectators (many of whom are wearing TEST MATCH SPECIAL radio-receiving hats): 'And a rather portly gentleman in a yellow – or would you call that orange, Foxy? – chemise is getting an enormous cheer. He's carrying a tray with five, no, six pints of beer. I dare say he'll be very popular when he finally arrives at his destination. And yes, well, jolly good luck to you, sir.'

And what can you say about this: 'I thought somebody was patting me on the head there. But I had merely leaned back into Christopher Martin-Jenkins's red notebook.'

Later, struggling to hear himself over parping noises,

he will lament, 'And someone in the crowd has got a motor horn. Oh dear.' Agnew, a TEST MATCH SPECIAL commentator since 1991, may insist that 'there are no stars on TMS', but it is difficult to think of Henry 'Blowers' Blofeld as anything but a star.

If Blofeld represents a florid, courteous era, the same could be said for Trevor Bailey ('The Boil'), who has been a summariser for more than two decades now. Bailey, like Fred Trueman and Vic Marks, is not on duty for this Test. However, he provided Peter Baxter with a classic TMS moment at Headingley in the 1970s. Bailey, socialising in the committee room, realised he was due on air to do the lunchtime summary. 'He ran out of the committee room,' Baxter smiles, 'and ran down the stairs, then ran up the stairs to the commentary box and finally arrived ... by which time he was too out of breath to speak. We had to fade him out.'

As for Trueman – he of the malfunctioning cigarette lighter and the inability to understand what is going off out there – Baxter recalls the occasion in the 1980s when F. S. T.'s amazing dexterity won him a round of applause from an entire commentary box. One of the famous TEST MATCH SPECIAL cakes, sent in by a listener, had been placed on a TV monitor in the box. Out of the corner of his eye, Trueman saw it slide off its perch. Swivelling on his chair, he caught the cake at ankle-height, earning an ovation that momentarily baffled the listeners. 'It was,' says Baxter, 'a sensational piece of fielding.'

If Trueman and Bailey are the voices of our childhoods and early adulthoods, then Agnew is probably BBC cricket's future. As a radio-lover and a cricket-lover, he is by necessity a forward-looking traditionalist. Blimpishly critical of Michael Atherton after the alleged ball-tampering episode against South Africa, he is by no

Henry Blofeld models what the well-dressed commentator will be wearing this year. No laughing at the back!

means conservative in outlook as a broadcaster. He is keen to make Radio 4's dial-twisting women listeners feel that TMS is their programme, too. And while he is critical of slow-motion replays and third umpires, he is in favour of developments such as Digital Audio Broadcasting, which could give TMS its own channel. 'It'll be tremendous for TMS. It'll be just like it used to be.'

He is referring, of course, to the golden years of TMS, when it had a safe home on Radio 3. On Radio 4 it has to tolerate the odd lodger, yielding to *The World At One* and the shipping forecast, perhaps the only two BBC radio institutions more hallowed than TMS itself.

Even on unfashionable long wave, it is impossible to calculate audience figures for TMS because it also goes out on World Service. The team receives letters from countries where cricket is not even played. A friend of Agnew's was walking along a street in Katmandu one day when he heard Aggers' voice coming out of a radio in a shop window.

Each time TMS has changed frequency, its listeners have changed their dials, or their radios, or their TMS hats, from medium wave to long wave. 'They have been amazingly loyal,' Agnew says, impressed. 'So patient.'

The irony is that, for all TMS's glorious heyday, Agnew himself scarcely heard any of it. He was playing cricket for a living, not listening to the radio. But he knows the history full well: the eight-hour marathons on Radio 3 that never dragged or bored; the rained-off days which turned into forums for debate, anecdote and fantasy. That particular luxury began to peter out when Radio 3's loss of its medium wave frequency forced TMS's move to Radio 5 in 1993, and has stopped altogether on Radio 4.

But every TMS fan remembers the halcyon summers on Radio 3: John Arlott, Brian Johnston, Trueman,

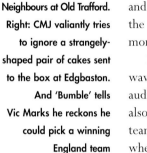

Below: Johnners watching Neighbours at Old Trafford. Right: CMJ valiantly tries to ignore a strangely-shaped pair of cakes sent to the box at Edgbaston. And 'Bumble' tells Vic Marks he reckons he could pick a winning England team

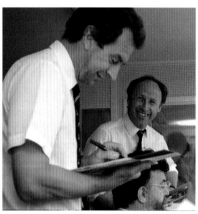

Bailey, Blofeld and Don Mosey. The mention of Mosey, a.k.a. 'The Alderman', causes a few awkward moments. Agnew and Baxter would rather not go into the ins and outs of it, but Mosey did, it transpires, blot his copybook with an indiscreet memoir, *The Alderman's Tale*, and has not been heard on TMS since 1991. One of Baxter's favourite memories of him dates back to a decade earlier, in Bombay, when visitors to the commentary box included Mike Gatting. 'Gatting was a fairly substantial young man,' Baxter says diplomatically. 'Don said, "Good morning, Mike." Gatting sat down, whereupon the chair immediately collapsed.'

Of Brian Johnston, however, everyone is delighted to reminisce. Both Baxter and Agnew (who was involved) cite the unforgettable hilarity of the 'legover' incident at The Oval in 1991. Baxter also has a warm memory of Johnston deflating the tension near the end of the Headingley Test in 1981 by reading out a listener's joke: 'Who were the two ice-cream sellers in the Bible? Lyons of Judah and Walls of Jericho.'

One element of Johnston's personality survives in the dormitory-style nicknames he bestowed on all TMS alumni. Blowers, Aggers, Bearders ... Johnston would even say 'clean-ers' when a batsman was clean bowled. He is also credited by Baxter with creating the mood of present-day TMS, with its listeners' letters, cakes and jokes. He kept listeners up-to-date with the plot of *Neighbours* ('Jim's tree has been cut down, that was the trouble') and he was delighted by streakers.

'Johnners made the programme what it is today, no doubt about it,' says Agnew. 'That's a tradition that hopefully will continue. I like to think little parts of him have rubbed off on all of us.'

Blofeld is reading out a letter on-air. But he is worried.

He knows – and Agnew knows he knows – that Agnew is a practical joker (as was Johnston) and he cannot rule out the possibility that Agnew has written the letter himself, booby-trapping it with obscenities. Then again, perhaps the letter itself will be harmless, except that the name underneath will be Ivor Biggun. Proceeding warily like a bomb disposal expert, Blofeld reads it line by line. It's harmless: a rather over-impressionistic cricket poem from a schoolboy called Daniel Thomas. Blofeld reads the first eight lines or so, before thanking Master Thomas kindly.

'David Lloyd was a great one for the letters,' Peter Baxter confides. 'On our fax machine we can stick things through to photocopy them and they look as though they've come by fax. You just sort of leave them on the machine: "Oh look, I think there's a fax for you…" Johnners interviewed a conductor one lunchtime who he'd actually never heard of. Bumble had "faxed" a whole lot of spurious details about him, like the fact that he kept ferrets and was known as "Ratty". Afterwards he sent us some CDs and signed them all Ratty.'

'I've had some great letters this summer,' Agnew reveals. 'I've had this running theme about my sister-in-law's horse that I couldn't catch. You know: got a phone call when I came back from the Edgbaston Test – "Go and catch this horse" – and I was in my best gear, jacket and tie, going through this bloody field trying to catch the horse and couldn't do it. And it's just gone on, about how I'm supposed to catch this horse. I've had brilliant suggestions from listeners.'

Even at this moment, the elongated, wafer-thin Christopher Martin-Jenkins ('The cricket purist of all of us,' says Agnew) is in the commentator's chair, reading out the latest in a series of faxes from listeners on the subject of aerodynamics, velocity and wing-spans. Neither he nor anyone else in the commentary box can recall how or why this correspondence began. But it is, they agree, far too late to stop it.

The same cannot be said for the Trent Bridge claret, which has run out, with no immediate plans to replace it. There are now five people crammed into the commentary box, for Graeme 'Foxy' Fowler has gone out to smoke a cigarette. Before he does that, though, he makes a quick phone call to Ronnie Scott's club in Nottingham. Fowler has friends playing there tonight: Tony Hadley and John Keeble, once the singer and drummer of Spandau Ballet.

In his light-fabric, strikingly lilac-coloured suit and psychedelically-designed tie, Fowler is sartorially somewhat at odds with his soberly-clad BBC colleagues. (The best-dressed man award must go to Ravi Shastri, BBC1's summariser, who looks immaculate in a dark suit.)

But then Fowler's an unusual fellow anyway. He didn't start smoking until he was 30 and he used to know Noel Gallagher of Oasis back in Manchester when Gallagher worked for the band Inspiral Carpets, with whom Fowler was friendly. He himself is a keen percussionist, once playing drums on an album called *Unhinged* by the veteran English folk singer Roy Harper.

The eccentric Fowler is nodding at something in the distance.

'They want to be getting a move on out there,' he says, exhaling Silk Cut smoke over the pavilion balcony as India's middle order potter along into the five-hundreds.

What's that? Oh, the cricket. Oh yes, they certainly want to be getting a move on.

'A friend of Agnew's was walking along a street in Katmandu one day when he heard Aggers' voice coming out of a radio in a shop window'

'This is brilliant, Aggers. With these TMS hats we can watch the game and still catch The Archers.' Below: the psychedelic Graeme Fowler

· TEST MATCH SPECIAL ·

Listeners' Poll

— Introduced by Phil McNeill, Editor —

TEST MATCH SPECIAL holds a unique place in its listeners' hearts. For us cricket followers, it is impossible to imagine the past 40 summers without Johnners, Blowers, Aggers and CMJ, Arlott, Trueman, Bailey and the Alderman, Tony Cozier, Vic Marks, Neville Oliver and all, chatting through the showers and illuminating the dramas of the finest of sports — exciting, amusing and infuriating by turns.

Like any fan of TMS, I have my favourites (the great Mr Bailey) and those who drive me mad (sorry, Vic — it's that laugh!). So I thought it would be fun to give other listeners the chance to express their views, by sending out poll forms to everyone who wrote in to TMS last year.

Thanks to the hundreds of people who took the time to reply. And apologies for any ruffled feathers!

Main picture – the TMS team in 1991, from left: Bill Frindall, Christopher Martin-Jenkins, Don Mosey, Fred Trueman, Tony Cozier, Brian Johnston, Trevor Bailey, Jonathan Agnew, Vic Marks, Peter Baxter, Mike Selvey

• BEST COMMENTATOR EVER •

1 **JOHN ARLOTT**

'His great gift was not simply bringing the cricket to you, but bringing you to the cricket'
Terence Christopher Coghlan, St Saviours, Jersey

2 BRIAN JOHNSTON

=3 JONATHAN AGNEW

=3 CHRISTOPHER MARTIN-JENKINS

5 ALAN MCGILVRAY
'The most impartial commentator I've ever heard'
Wendy Gardner, Cardiff

6 REX ALSTON

7 HENRY BLOFELD

8 E. W. SWANTON

9 RICHIE BENAUD

=10 TREVOR BAILEY

=10 TONY COZIER

• BEST CRICKET BRAIN IN THE BOX •

1 **TREVOR BAILEY**
'Unsurpassed in any sport'
Trevor English, Maidstone, Kent

2 CHRISTOPHER MARTIN-JENKINS
'Knowledge backed by a deep love of cricket'
Don Gerrard, Cowbridge, Vale of Glamorgan

3 BILL FRINDALL

4 DAVID LLOYD
'Better in the commentary box than the dressing room!'
P. Mann, Ravenshead, Notts

=5 JONATHAN AGNEW

=5 GEOFFREY BOYCOTT
'Ask him and he'll tell you himself!'
Max Chadwick, Stoke-on-Trent

=5 VIC MARKS

=8 E. W. SWANTON

=8 FRED TRUEMAN

10 HENRY BLOFELD

• BEST SENSE OF HUMOUR •

1 **BRIAN JOHNSTON**

'Childish, I know, but captivating'

D. T. J. Willbie, Dunstable, Beds

2 JONATHAN AGNEW

'His bubbly personality is infectious. His joyous involvement rubs off on us all'

Don Gerrard, Cowbridge, Vale of Glamorgan

3 HENRY BLOFELD

'Not only witty himself, but "the cause that wit is in other men"!'

M. C. Ellis, Leatherhead, Surrey

4 DAVID LLOYD

5 VIC MARKS

'That engaging chuckle'

P. Mann, Ravenshead, Notts

6 GRAEME FOWLER

7 JOHN ARLOTT

8 TREVOR BAILEY

'Very, very dry'

Stephen Keach, Attleborough, Norfolk

9 BILL FRINDALL

=10 DON MOSEY

=10 FRED TRUEMAN

• FAVOURITE VOICE •

1 **JOHN ARLOTT**

'His voice was cricket: summer days in the West Country on the village green'

Don Gerrard, Cowbridge, Vale of Glamorgan

2 HENRY BLOFELD

3 JONATHAN AGNEW

4 BRIAN JOHNSTON

5 CHRISTOPHER MARTIN-JENKINS

6 DAVID LLOYD

7 TREVOR BAILEY

=8 FRED TRUEMAN

=8 TONY COZIER

=8 ALAN MCGILVRAY

'A warm, light-hearted, amusing, loving voice'

Rhoda Meldrum, Newcastle-upon-Tyne

• MOST IRRITATING •

1 **FRED TRUEMAN**

'But where would we be without "I don't know what's going off out there"'

Leslie Wakerell, London W14

2 TREVOR BAILEY

3 HENRY BLOFELD

'I like cricket, not buses!'

Malcolm Rees, Epsom, Surrey

4 GEOFFREY BOYCOTT

5 DAVID LLOYD

6 DON MOSEY

7 CHRISTOPHER MARTIN-JENKINS

8 BRIAN JOHNSTON

9 JEREMY CONEY

10 VIC MARKS

'That infuriating snigger'

R. Brent, Woodford Green, Essex

• MOST MISSED •

1 **BRIAN JOHNSTON**

'Because he never had a bad word to say about anyone'

R. Howarth, Bridport, Dorset

2 JOHN ARLOTT

'Hearing his commentary was like looking at a moving picture'

Sandra Wilson, Kirkcaldy

3 ALAN MCGILVRAY

4 DON MOSEY

5 JIM LAKER

• FAVOURITE CRICKETER •

1 **IAN BOTHAM**

'Not for just his skill, but for his generosity of spirit when others do well'

Mrs P. Dawes, Eastbourne

2 GARY SOBERS

3 DAVID GOWER

'The golden boy with the glam'

Rhoda Meldrum, Newcastle-upon-Tyne

4 DEREK RANDALL

'For the way he stood up to Lillee and Thomson at the MCG in 1977'

Graham Phillips, Midhurst, West Sussex

5 DENIS COMPTON

'The sun came out when he appeared'

Michael Flynn, Burton-on-Trent

=6 COLIN COWDREY

=6 VIV RICHARDS

=8 TOM GRAVENEY

=8 CLIVE LLOYD

=10 GEOFFREY BOYCOTT

=10 GRAHAM GOOCH

=10 JACK RUSSELL

=10 PETER MAY

From top: Christopher Martin-Jenkins, Jonathan Agnew, and Geoffrey Boycott – who figures in the lists for both Most Irritating Commentator and Favourite Cricketer

John & Johnners

JOHN ARLOTT DIED ON
14 DECEMBER 1991,
BRIAN JOHNSTON
ON 5 JANUARY 1994.
TIM RICE REFLECTS
ON TWO MEN
WHOSE VOICES STILL
ECHO WHEREVER
CRICKET IS PLAYED

John Arlott and Brian Johnston – two giants of broadcasting, both forever primarily associated with TEST MATCH SPECIAL, wide though their talents spread in other areas both in and apart from radio. Now, as we celebrate forty years of this remarkable British sporting institution, with neither of these voices a part of the mellifluous mix, it is hard to believe that Arlott has been away from the microphone for nearly two decades and that 1997 will be the fourth summer without Johnners, who more or less died in harness. So resonant are their contrasting powers of articulation and communication that one still expects Jonathan Agnew, Henry Blofeld or Christopher Martin-Jenkins to be handing over to John or Brian in a few overs' time.

Both men were born just before the First World War. With impeccable timing, Brian actually came into this world on the first day of an England-Australia match at Lord's. The three-day game was part of the ill-fated Triangular Test Tournament of 1912, in which the cricketing authorities, decades ahead of their time, boldly attempted to organise a tripartite Test series between the only powers of the day – England, Australia and South Africa. Dire weather, an Australian team weakened by internal strife that led to many of their stars boycotting the tour, and a sub-standard South African team all contributed to the failure of the bold experiment. So maybe it is not stretching it to say that the most significant cricketing moment of that summer was the arrival of the infant B. A. Johnston on 24 June, though Jack Hobbs's masterful 107 on that very day must run it close.

John Arlott was born two years later, on 25 February 1914. No Test Match was actually in

by Sir Tim Rice (RIGHT, WITH JOHNNERS AT THE LORD'S MUSEUM)

'On the surface they were different breeds: the Liberal and the Conservative, the serious and the light-hearted, the poet and the entertainer, the wines and the cakes, the countryman and the Etonian. But both were driven by a strong sense of morality and dedicated to the values that cricket is still sometimes able to inspire'

– SIR TIM RICE

• JOHNSTON ON ARLOTT •

'You could smell bat oil when he spoke and picture the village green with its thatched pub and all the players in their flannels.'

• JOHNNERS ON ARLOTT •

'I've got this awful schoolboyish sense of humour. Dear old John Arlott, with his wit and delightful descriptive style, never really approved.'

• ARLOTT ON ARLOTT •

'I've been able to devote my life to three things people appreciate – poetry, cricket and wine. That's bloody lucky.'

• DYLAN THOMAS ON THE ARLOTT STYLE •

'Exact, enthusiastic, prejudiced, amazingly visual, authoritative and friendly.'

• IAN BOTHAM ON ARLOTT •

'There will never be another John Arlott. He was TEST MATCH SPECIAL. He will always be.'

progress that day, but the England team were touring South Africa, an appropriate, or perhaps ironic, venue to find the national side at the time of Arlott's birth. It was the tour when S. F. Barnes swept all before him, taking no less than 49 wickets in just four Tests, still a world record for any bowler in any rubber of any size. John Arlott's relationship with South Africa was to be a turbulent one; on his one visit there in 1948-9 following

What a sweetie! Brian Johnston at work and, right, showing off the ever-present two-tone shoes while watching England play Pakistan at Old Trafford in 1992

George Mann's side, his eyes were opened to the indignities and cruelties of apartheid and he never went back. He announced he would not commentate on their (ultimately cancelled) 1970 tour of England. It is sad that he did not live to see the final dismantling of the system he abhorred.

John Arlott's final Test in the TMS seat was the 1980 Centenary match between England and Australia at Lord's, a game marred by an altercation between MCC members and an umpire, but more happily remembered for the

brief cessation of play on the final afternoon as the entire crowd stood and players downed tools to mark the end of an era as John's ultimate commentary ended with typical lack of flamboyance from the hero himself.

Brian's final stint in front of the microphone (which no one knew then would be his swan song) was also an England-Australia Test – the Oval game of 1993 in which Brian was able to sign off reporting on a rare England victory after a long summer of disappointment.

• JOHNNERS ON TMS •

'We're like any group of friends that goes to a cricket or
rugger match. We sit together, swap jokes, and
if someone has a good tale he's encouraged to tell it.
We like a glass of something, but not a lot.
We are professionals.
Most importantly, we all think that cricket is fun.
Do you know, in all my time I've never had a quarrel in the
box. Strange, really, when you think we're all extroverts.
Take Fred Trueman. You couldn't get a much greater contrast
than him and me, yet we get on like a house on fire.'

• ARLOTT ON AN AUSTRALIAN FAST BOWLER •

'Consider Lillee in the field.
He toils, but he does not spin.'

• JOHNNERS ON MARRIAGE •

'I understand there are some men who
do not like cricket, but I would not like my
daughter to marry one.'

'Brian was a friend to those who never knew
him and eyes to those who cannot see.'

– BLIND CRICKET FAN MELVIN COLLINS –
at Brian Johnston's memorial service at Westminster Abbey

On the surface the two were different breeds: the Liberal and the Conservative, the serious and the light-hearted, the poet and the entertainer, the wines and the cakes, the countryman and the Etonian.

But both were driven by a strong sense of morality and dedication to the values that cricket is still sometimes able to inspire: the service of the individual to the greater good of the many, the bringing together of widely disparate cultures through a common enthusiasm, fair play and recognition through a great game that there are yet more important struggles beyond the boundary.

Both voices are unforgettable. First the Hampshire burr and then the public school tones became the voice of English cricket – one might have expected the order to

• ARLOTT'S FINAL COMMENTARY •

‘*28 Boycott, 15 Gower, 69 for two.*
And after a few comments from Trevor Bailey
it'll be Christopher Martin-Jenkins.’

have been reversed as we move towards a classless sound on the airwaves. Cricket has, however, more individuality than most walks of English life. Just as Arlott's rich rural accent was the exception in his early broadcasting years, so Johnston's courtly fluency was an unusual feature of radio in his later years. But they both triumphed over the fashions of the day by their command of the English language and their ability to communicate with honesty and enthusiasm.

It is of course a resounding tribute to TEST MATCH SPECIAL that it continues as lustily as ever with a line-up that was barely out of short trousers (or even nappies in at least one case) when it was first aired in 1957. But without the genius of Arlott and Johnston this might not have been the case.

Left: John Arlott waves goodbye to Headingley. Soon after his final commentary at Lord's, a message arrived from the MCC inviting him to lunch. He just growled: 'Why now? They've never asked me before.'

• A JOHNNERS CLASSIC •
In an England v New Zealand match in 1969, Glenn Turner was hit in the box with the fifth ball of the over. 'It looks as if he's going to try and continue,' said Brian, 'though he still looks very shaken and pale. Very plucky of him. Yes, he's definitely going to have a try. One ball left.'

• DAVID GOWER ON JOHNNERS •
‘*He was the last of the gentleman commentators, his voice and sense of humour instantly recognisable and not just to cricket lovers. Professional cricketers can be highly sensitive, but none of them could ever have been wounded by Johnners on air. Whenever I joined the TMS team, I was struck by the easy working atmosphere – a tribute to them all but especially to Brian, whose great gift was to be able to communicate in a relaxed and friendly fashion. My lasting appreciation of Johnners was the card I received from him on passing Geoffrey Boycott's then England Test Match run record. It said simply: 'Gratters, Johnners'.*’

• MIKE BREARLEY ON ARLOTT •
‘*John brought the eye and tongue of a poet; the accent and timbre of a Hampshire grave-digger's son; and the courage to describe a whole scene, to give a rich game its setting. He knew cricket more in the way of the lover than of the critic and, as such, tended to romanticise the performers.*’

Champagne Moments

LISTENERS AND COMMENTATORS RECALL THEIR FAVOURITE INCIDENTS FROM 40 YEARS OF TEST MATCH SPECIAL

The moment I remember most vividly is more of a poignant moment than a champagne one. It was John Arlott's last commentary, when at the end of his stint at the microphone, without fuss or ballyhoo, he simply finished by saying: 'And after Trevor Bailey it will be Christopher Martin-Jenkins.' With those few undemonstrative words, the 'voice of cricket' simply was no more.

— Terence Christopher Coghlan, St Saviours, Jersey

For me the Champagne Moment comes on the first day of every Test Match, when the TMS team say 'Good morning'. With that comes that wonderful tingle of a Test Match beginning, five days of sheer pleasure stretching ahead. Needless to say, the saddest is part is the last day of the last Test. The radio falls quiet and I have to join the real(?) world again.

— Audrey Amor, Olney, Bucks

TEST MATCH SPECIAL
Quiz

• **THE SEVENTIES** •

5   Which England bowler took advantage of Fusarium Oxysporum to bowl Australia out?

Answer on page 120

HENRY BLOFELD'S CHAMPAGNE MOMENT

Bowled over by a maiden

'In-house' Champagne Moments have been less frequent since Johnners died, but we do our best. My favourite happened in 1995, in a Test Match against the West Indies at The Oval.

Vic Marks (in that inimitable linen jacket of his which is a Champagne Moment all on its own) was sharing the commentary with me. Suddenly we were given cups of coffee, and I showed my appreciation on air.

Sir Everton Weekes, who had just been knighted and was one of our experts, told me from the back of the box that it had been very remiss of me not to tell listeners that we had been given coffee by a spectacularly beautiful girl. He was referring to our friend Shilpa Patel, who works for the BBC and always looks as if she is about to win the Miss World title.

So I added: 'Everton Weekes tells me it was remiss of me not to have told listeners that we had been given our coffee by a very lovely girl.'

As I did this, I looked round and saw Shilpa handing a cup to Everton. 'My goodness me,' I piped up, 'she's giving Everton one too!'

Whenever Brian Johnston met up with cake he was in his element. Whatever type of cake it was, whoever the sender, whatever condition it arrived in, Johnners devoured it with gusto, and one cannot help thinking it was this (along with John Arlott's favourite beaujolais) that inspired his commentary. Would we have had moments of magic like 'The bowler's Holding, the batman's Willey' without it? I think not.

— David Wickens, Bishops Stortford, Herts

Henry Blofeld, 1996: 'He walks back. Looks at the ball as though it's about to explode. It doesn't. He bowls and there's no run.'

— Robin Millar, London W6

My first Champagne Moment involves Ian Botham, a set of stumps, Brian Johnston and Jonathan Agnew. My second is a song Brian Johnston used to sing about 'A Little Sausage'.

— Paul Johnston, Penrith, Cumbria

John Arlott was in brilliant form in covering Clive Lloyd's magnificent hundred in the 1975 World Cup Final. He said it was 'not how difficult to bowl a maiden over but to bowl a maiden ball', and then as Lloyd moved effortlessly to 99 with a four over midwicket, delivered the perfect phrase, describing 'the stroke of a man knocking a thistle top off with a walking stick'.

A Champagne Moment indeed!

— *Robin Osmond, Hawkesbury, Gloucs*

The last Ashes series in England. A young Aussie opener, probably Slater, scored a century. He correctly acknowledged the applause from all sides of the ground – generously given for a good knock from a young man – then kissed his cap.

There was no affectation, no 'side', no attempt to pose for the cameras … just a young man recognising the importance of the moment both for himself and for his country.

It showed that, even in these times of 'professional' sport, people can still appreciate that a sporting event has worth because of its sporting context, not because it may bring monetary gain.

— *Jeremy Gibbon, Bradford*

BILL FRINDALL'S CHAMPAGNE MOMENT

Kapil's four-ball fanfare

Of the many Champagne Moments in my 31 summers with TMS, my favourite involves Kapil Dev's world record during 'Graham Gooch's Match' – the First Test between England and India at Lord's in 1990.

India still needed 24 to avert the follow-on when Kapil was joined by last man Narendra Hirwani. Eddie Hemmings bowled from the Nursery End, tossing the ball up invitingly. Kapil studiously blocked the first two balls before straight-driving the remaining four into the building site of the Compton and Edrich stands.

The fourth six took India to safety and set a record for the most consecutive sixes in a Test Match. It was a sensational solution to the problem of the follow-on – and his bemused partner was out next ball.

GRAEME FOWLER'S CHAMPAGNE MOMENT

Arkle overdoes it

Derek Randall at deep square leg dived full length and caught an unbelievable catch at Lord's. By way of celebration he threw the ball over his shoulder – but it went backwards a little too far and struck a spectator straight on the forehead, rendering the poor gentleman senseless.

The sight of the crowd clustered round this prostrate gentleman with Derek bent over him saying 'Sorry, sorry, sorry' is a scene I'll never forget.

During 1977 I was commuting by car from Watford to Sevenoaks. The journey was grim, being pre-M25. The drive home was frustrating to say the least – but was lightened considerably during the summer months by listening to TEST MATCH SPECIAL.

On one occasion, 11 August, the unthinkable happened – the Test Match had reached a point where Geoffrey Boycott was batting but I didn't want him to score another run, at least not just yet. He was facing Greg Chappell and I was about to enter the Blackwall Tunnel, in which of course all radio contact would be lost.

Into the Tunnel I went, cursing all the other drivers for holding me back and convinced that I would miss the imminent Champagne Moment of the Season.

I emerged on the north side of the Thames at 5.48pm and 30 seconds to discover, with immense relief, that Boycott had not scored another run.

My prayer had been answered and, from the very next ball, he on-drove Chappell to the boundary to complete his 100th first-class hundred.

Robert Little, Yeovil, Somerset

LORD (BRIAN) RIX: My Champagne Moment came in June 1982, during the Lord's Test Match, when I was invited on to the TMS View from the Boundary. It was the lunchtime filler, but rain had stopped play, so I rabbited on quite happily for nearly two hours along with Brian Johnston, Fred Trueman and Don Mosey. Gosh, I envy the commentators their job. Imagine watching all the Test Matches from a prime position, being fed and watered and, furthermore, being paid to do it. Some people have all the luck!

TEST MATCH SPECIAL
Quiz
• THE SEVENTIES •

6 Which England batsman was described after his first Test appearance as 'a bank clerk going to war'?

Answer on page 120

TMS ball by ball

TEST MATCH SPECIAL
COMMENTATORS RECALL
MATCHES THAT MADE HISTORY
SINCE THE FIRST BROADCAST
IN 1957 – COMPLETE WITH
COMMENTARY AS IT HAPPENED

May and Cowdrey rewrite the record books

The first ever TEST MATCH SPECIAL, *and one of the most remarkable, as Peter May and Colin Cowdrey escaped from Sonny Ramadhin's clutches with a world record partnership of 411. Trevor Bailey witnessed every ball – with his pads on*

ENGLAND v WEST INDIES

EDGBASTON, 30 MAY-4 JUNE 1957

England 186	*S. Ramadhin 7-49*
W. Indies 474	*O. G. Smith 161, C. L. Walcott 90,*
	F. M. M. Worrell 81, G. St A. Sobers 53
England 583-4 dec	*P. B. H. May 285*, M. C. Cowdrey 154*
W. Indies 72-7	
	Match drawn (England won the series 3-0)

A lthough I never contributed less in any Test than in the opening one of the 1957 series against the West Indies – the first to be staged at Edgbaston for 28 years, and the first broadcast under the banner of TEST MATCH SPECIAL – it still took more out of me than any other.

Having won the toss on a very good pitch, Peter May elected to bat, only for England to be mesmerised by that little magician 'Sonny' Ramadhin, who took seven for 49. I was bowled by 'Sonny' for a solitary single.

KEN ABLACK: *'The field being set for Bailey, Ramadhin's having a word with Goddard. The offside field is now one slip, a man at point square with the wicket, cover and mid-off. 116 for four. Ramadhin to Bailey, shorter, and that one off the inside edge. Sobers throws himself across to the*

Left: Colin Cowdrey and Peter May take a well-earned break from their labours

left, gets a hand to it, Ramadhin holds his head. Gerry Gomez, was that a catch?'

GERRY GOMEZ: *'No, it dropped short of him Ken, off the inside edge – a quicker one.'*

KEN ABLACK: *'Now Ramadhin again to Bailey, Bailey forward and he's bowled!'*

GERRY GOMEZ: *'It was an off-spinner flighted much slower than the previous ball, and Bailey ... frankly, having played against Bailey quite a few times, I've never seen him more conclusively bowled than on this occasion. I think that Bailey will admit that it's one of the better balls that he has received in his career. He was beaten in the flight where he started moving forward to the pitch of it but never got there and it hit the off stump. It was a beautiful piece of bowling by Ramadhin, a beautiful variation of pace from the previous ball, and this innings so far is all Ramadhin on a wicket which I don't think is yet his piece of cake really.'*

KEN ABLACK: *'Well, what a dramatic change. England 93 for two at lunch, now 116 for five. Ramadhin right on top.'*

We were dismissed for a miserable 186. The West Indies replied with a formidable 474, in which Collie Smith struck a splendid 161, and my figures were 0 for 80. Despite a better start to our second innings, at 113 for three including two more wickets to Ramadhin, an innings defeat was plainly the logical outcome. As a

Recalled by Trevor Bailey

The three commentators for the first TMS were John Arlott, Ken Ablack and Rex Alston, with summarisers Bill Bowes and Gerry Gomez, and close-of-play summaries by E. W. Swanton

E. W. Swanton was in the commentary box for the first ever TEST MATCH SPECIAL

My predominant recollections of the match are threefold. There was the tactic whereby England sought to counter the spin of Ramadhin, and the negative acceptance of the changing situation by the West Indian captain. Brighter in my mind than the long drawn-out battle on the field is the memory of sitting on the open top of the Pavilion containing the broadcasting box listening along with Ian Peebles to the oracle, greatest of all bowlers, S. F. Barnes. I was fascinated by his large, strong hands and the long fingers with which he spun and cut and swung the ball at will. At 84 I believe that the Staffordshire County Council was still employing him for his copper-plate writing.

Out in the middle Sonny Ramadhin's fingers grew more and more tired as he spun over after over – a record of 129 of them in all – most of them against the broad bats of Peter May and Colin Cowdrey. Uncertain about the direction of his spin, they decided always to play for an off-break, thrusting forward, bat and pad together. Their stand of 411 for the fourth wicket (another world record) was an epic of concentration and endurance.

It has to be said, though, that John Goddard smoothed their paths by setting a defensive field even at the start of the partnership when England were still 175 behind. He allowed 162 overs to be bowled with the second new ball, and he continued to bowl Ramadhin to the bitter end.

The scourge of England in past series was never again the same bowler.

Right: Rohan Kanhai whips off the bails but Cowdrey survives.
Below: Sonny Ramadhin, who bowled a world record number of overs

player I was never an avid watcher when my side were batting, unless there was something very exciting and special happening or I wanted to study a particular bowler. However, when it was my turn to go in next, I naturally watched very intently, as it does help to know

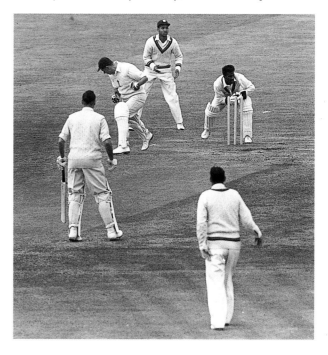

whom you will be facing and what they are bowling.

With Essex my wait was frequently brief, but this was not to be the case at Edgbaston, as Peter May and Colin Cowdrey embarked upon a massive stand of 411 runs and 'Sonny' sent down 98 overs while I sat there quietly in the same spot with my pads on and gloves and bat adjacent for hour after hour and session after session except, after each appeal, when I half rose to my feet.

As both batsmen employed their front pad as a defensive barrier every time Ramadhin pitched fractionally outside the off stump, I estimate there must have been close upon 100 unsuccessful shouts. Rohan Kanhai, who was making his international debut as well as keeping wicket, reckoned that only about ten were plumb.

REX ALSTON: *'And England must be looking for runs now. Smith bowls short, Cowdrey has placed it gently towards third*

man, and the extra applause is because the partnership is now worth a monumental figure of 400. I think the imagination starts to boggle at all this business about records. We're getting tired of it, I should think Roy Webber is drooling records somewhere else along in this box. There must have been higher records. What is the highest partnership? Now, Jack Price, here's a problem for you: What's the highest partnership by a couple of Englishmen in a Test Match in England? You can work that one out quietly, while Sobers starts the fresh over with the score 513 for three.

'And Sobers bowls to Cowdrey, and he draws away and forces it off the back foot, and Ramadhin fields very deep at third man. One run to Cowdrey; he's now scored 153…

'And now May, 247, faces Sobers and May has hit the next one high in the air! It's six, into the Pavilion just over mid-on, and he's also scored a mere 250, 253 to be precise…

'Sobers bowls to him again and May has waited for that, which was a half-volley, very well pitched-up and very wide of the off stump, and May flashes the bat and it goes to Ramadhin at third man. May 254, England 521 for three.'

Like so many cricketers, I was superstitious, and I believed that to move from my chosen position in the dressing room was bound to be unlucky – with the result that after four sessions I felt as if I had entered a time vacuum, and was very thankful that when that great partnership ended I did not have to go to the crease, because I am quite sure I would never have found my way out to the middle, as well as being completely exhausted.

Not surprisingly in the circumstances, our eventual declaration was somewhat overdue and, as so often occurs in this type of situation, the West Indies collapsed. At close of play Trueman, Lock and Laker had them struggling on 72 for seven and I was not required to bowl a ball or take a catch.

I left that evening for Essex feeling somewhat depressed by my failure to make runs or take wickets, and not for one moment imagining that I would capture 11 in the next Test. The strange thing is that I can remember Edgbaston far more clearly than victory at Lord's.

Peter May follows a ball down the leg side during his marathon innings of 285 not out

The battle of Cowdrey's broken arm

Colin Cowdrey played many key innings for England –
but none more vital than the day he stepped out ready to face
the fury of Wes Hall with his left arm in plaster

ENGLAND v WEST INDIES
LORD'S, 20-25 JUNE 1963

W. Indies 301	*R. B. Kanhai 73, J. S. Solomon 56;*
	F. S. Trueman 6-100
England 297	*K. F. Barrington 80, E. R. Dexter 70,*
	F. J. Titmus 52*; C. C. Griffith 5-91
W. Indies 229	*B. F. Butcher 133; F. S. Trueman 5-52*
England 228-9	*D. B. Close 70, K. F. Barrington 60*
Match drawn	*(West Indies won the series 3-1)*

This was certainly the most dramatic Test Match in which I was involved as a broadcaster. In statistical terms, England's heroes were Ken Barrington, who made 80 and 60, and Ted Dexter, who set the ground alight with a scintillating 70 in 81 minutes, while Fred Trueman took the bowling honours with eleven wickets in the match. But the final hero was Colin Cowdrey.

The West Indies made 301 in their first innings, Rohan Kanhai being the top scorer with 73. This proved enough to give them a lead of four runs as the fearsome Charlie Griffith took five England wickets for 91. The second West Indies innings was held together by Basil Butcher's 133.

Set 234 to win, England faced a ferocious attack by Hall and Griffith. Only Barrington and Brian Close, with a gallant 70 runs and as many bruises on his body, made more than 20, and to add to England's troubles

Recalled by Robert Hudson

Colin Cowdrey, arm in plaster, walks out to bat, prepared to face Wes Hall left-handed

Cowdrey was hit by a short ball from Wes Hall and had to retire on 19 with a broken arm.

It was Hall who bowled the last over. With three balls remaining, the score was 228 for nine. The batsman was Derek Shackleton, who had been brought into the side at the age of 38 in place of Brian Statham...

ALAN GIBSON: *'Six runs are needed and three balls are left. A feverish atmosphere now as Hall comes in and bowls to Shackleton. Shackleton flashes outside the off stump, doesn't get a touch, and they go through for a very quick single ... and Shackleton's going to be run out! He's run out.'*

All eyes turned to the Pavilion to see if the wounded Cowdrey would come out to bat.

ALAN GIBSON: *'228 for nine. They are not coming in. We must therefore presume that with two balls to go Cowdrey will come in. And the applause seems to me to indicate that Cowdrey is coming out – and the cheering tells you that in fact he is. There are two balls to go. Cowdrey, his left forearm in plaster, coming out to join Allen.'*

Cowdrey planned to bat left-handed – though fortunately the batsmen had crossed during the run-out and it was the No. 10, David Allen, who would receive the next ball.

ALAN GIBSON: *'The crowd now swarming out of the stands, the West Indians particularly coming up eagerly right round the boundary rope waiting to charge on to the field as soon as this dramatic and gripping Test has ended. And end it is bound to, either in the next ball or the one after that.*

'Here comes the first of them, Hall bowls to Allen, and Allen plays it out to the off side and there is no run...

'And Wesley Hall is going to bowl the last ball of the match from the Pavilion End. He comes in and bowls it, and Allen plays defensively and the match is drawn. The crowd come swarming on to the field. Cowdrey does not have to play a ball. The ground staff, the policemen are desperately rushing out to protect the sacred middle. The West Indies cricketers being chased in by their own enthusiastic supporters, Wesley Hall, still with a tremendous run in him, leading the rush off the field. The end of a great game of cricket.'

No draw was ever more exciting!

Above: Cowdrey paces the balcony outside the dressing room, wondering if he will need to bat.
Left: The match is drawn and Cowdrey leads the way as the players run for cover

Fiery Fred's 300th

It seemed an impossible feat at the time.
But when England's greatest fast bowler took his 300th wicket,
all he could think about was his 301st

ENGLAND v AUSTRALIA

THE OVAL, 13-18 AUGUST 1964

England 182	N. J. N. Hawke 6-47
Australia 379	W. M. Lawry 94, B. C. Booth 74,
	T. R. Vievers 67*; F. S. Trueman 4-87
England 381-4	G. Boycott 113, M. C. Cowdrey 93*,
	F. J. Titmus 56, K. F. Barrington 54*
Match drawn	*(Australia won the series 1-0)*

If all the people who say they were there at The Oval on Saturday 15 August 1964 really were, there must have been something like a million in the crowd, judging by the letters I have received.

That year I had got four wickets against Australia in the Third Test at Headingley, but had been dropped for the Fourth, when there were huge scores at Old Trafford – a triple hundred from Simpson and a double by Barrington in reply. When I missed that Test, I thought I would also miss the chance to get the three wickets I needed to become the first man to take 300 Test wickets. But I was back in the side for the final Test at The Oval.

England had been bowled out for 182 on the first day and Australia batted through the second, when I had Bill Lawry dropped. By late Saturday morning, as the Australian lead grew, Ted Dexter, our captain, was looking a little bemused as to who to put on to bowl before

Recalled by Fred Trueman

Fred Trueman leads the England team off after becoming the first bowler to take 300 wickets

lunch. He was thinking of trying my old pal Peter Parfitt. I thought, I'm not having this – and so I took the ball off the captain and said, 'I'll bowl'.

So I put myself on at the Pavilion End and was lucky to get one to nip back and knock Redpath's off stump back. Graham McKenzie came in and first ball I got one to hold up which he nicked through to Colin Cowdrey at first slip. So I was on 299 wickets and on a hat-trick.

The next man in was an old pal, Neil Hawke, who told me he was halfway down the stairs when they told him it was lunchtime and we were coming off. I sat in the dressing room after I'd changed my shirt and socks, having a sandwich and a cup of tea, trying to concentrate and pondering that I might soon make history by becoming the first man to take 300 Test wickets.

Neil Hawke had said to me, 'If I'm your 300th wicket we'll have a drink together, because that's the only way I'm going to be remembered in the history of the game.' And we'd just laughed about it.

The hat-trick ball, the first ball after lunch, was wide outside the off stump. But then the new ball became available and I thought, Now I've got to try to get this in the right place. And eventually I did.

JOHN ARLOTT: *'Trueman with a bit of a scowl at the batsman. Doesn't even look friendly towards his fieldsmen at the moment. In his 31st over. Has two wickets. Wants a third. Trueman in again. Bowls to Hawke — and Hawke goes forward and is caught! There's the 300th! There was no nicer touch than Trueman congratulating Hawke. Caught by Cowdrey!*

'Neil Hawke can never have come into the pavilion to a greater ovation in his life — but they weren't looking at him. Fred Trueman's 300th Test wicket. The first man in the history of cricket to achieve the figure when Hawke played a half-hearted stroke outside the off stump to a ball that took the outside edge and Cowdrey swooped on it, two hands. It was high in the air, up went Trueman, up went the crowd, stood to him, cheered him, and as Hawke walked away Trueman congratulated him.'

JACK FINGLETON: *'A nice neat catch by Cowdrey and my heartfelt congratulations, as an Australian, to one of the*

greatest fighters we've ever had against us. This chap is never beaten. He's put everything into the game and it couldn't have happened to a greater fighter. Well done, Freddie Trueman.'

Funnily enough, I didn't feel anything really apart from the congratulations of my team-mates. What I was thinking about was that Graham Corling was coming in and if I got that wicket it would be 301. And I did – Peter Parfitt caught him at slip.

It was only afterwards that it sank in what I had done. That was really my first introduction to TEST MATCH SPECIAL, because I went up to the box, where John Arlott spoke to me, and I said that if anyone else got 300 Test wickets they would be very tired.

A well-earned bath: Fred celebrates by signalling his three-oh-one.
Top: Colin Cowdrey throws the ball high in the air after taking the catch off Neil Hawke (left) that gave Trueman his 300th Test wicket

Congdon's doomed assault on Everest

It was a mountain of runs: 479 to win. And New Zealand had never beaten England, let alone after such a disastrous start. From the other side of the world, Bryan Waddle listened, gripped, as they so very nearly reached the top...

A moment of crisis as Bev Congdon is hit on the jaw by a bouncer from John Snow. He recovered to bat all the next day

ENGLAND v NEW ZEALAND

TRENT BRIDGE, 7-12 JUNE 1973

England 250	G. Boycott 51;
	D. R. Hadlee 4-42, B. R. Taylor 4-53
New Zealand 97	A. W. Greig 4-33
England 325-8 dec	A. W. Greig 139, D. L. Amiss 138
New Zealand 440	B. E. Congdon 176, V. Pollard 116;
	G. G. Arnold 5-131

England won by 38 runs

(England won the series 2-0)

'England won by 38 runs' was the bald fact of the First Test of the 1973 series, but behind that result lay a match of courage and tenacity from a New Zealand side that was ultimately denied. After a feeble first-innings total of 97 had left New Zealand 153 behind, Dennis Amiss and Tony Greig both scored centuries to set NZ a daunting 479 to win. Yet they so nearly got there.

Bevan Congdon had been hit in the face on the third evening by a ball from John Snow, casting doubt on his ability to continue batting. But the NZ captain produced a dogged, determined innings that almost won the Test. He and Vic Pollard took New Zealand to 307 for four with an inspirational fifth-wicket partnership of 177.

ALAN RICHARDS: *'New Zealand 307 for four. There have been 727 official Tests in the history of cricket, and this is only the 33rd time that 300 runs have been scored by the team batting fourth. So New Zeland have achieved something.*

'Here's Arnold, goes in again, bowls to Congdon — and he's bowled him! He's got through Congdon's defensive shot, and Arnold has struck the blow that England had been waiting so long for. Congdon, bowled Arnold, 176. And how disappointed he must be, with the clock showing only 13 minutes remaining today, to be coming back a tired man, having batted all day. How dearly he would have loved to stay and fight out the remainder of the innings. 176 to

Recalled by Bryan Waddle

Bevan Congdon, his top score in Test cricket.'

NORMAN YARDLEY: *'It certainly has been a magnificent perform-ance against the odds. He's had his little bit of luck, but who gets 176 and doesn't have a little bit of luck?'*

With Pollard batting as if his life depended on it, New Zealand still had a chance…

ALAN RICHARDS: *'The sun is with us now, it's quite breezy, the wind*

As Vic Pollard (left) and Bev Congdon (below) put on 177 runs together to take New Zealand to 307 for four, an improbable victory seemed to be within their grasp

blowing across the ground from square leg through point. 367 for five. Pollard is 99, seeking his first Test century and his fifth only in first-class cricket. Here's Greig, he bowls now to Pollard. Pollard plays him in front of his stumps, they're going for the quick single. Greig tried to effect the run-out — they're through, he's made it!

'Vic Pollard has his first Test century. If he makes any more, not many of them will be better than this one. Pollard 100 and his hundred has come in 372 minutes — that's over six hours.'

Pollard and Ken Wadsworth took the score on to 402. Half a day to get 77 runs, with five wickets in hand.

JOHN ARLOTT: *'77 they now want with five wickets to fall, and Arnold bowls to Wadsworth and he edges it and he's magnificently caught. He is quite splendidly caught by Roope going far, far to his right at second slip, and let me say there are not more than three or four people in English cricket today who would have caught that. It must have been at least six feet wide of his right foot as he stood at second slip and he got across, took it two-handed. Bill Frindall reminds me that he's a goalkeeper. He took it*

two-handed, goalkeeper fashion, away wide to his right, and Wadsworth is short of the fifty that would have come if that had been missed. Caught Roope, bowled Arnold, 46. 402 for six — and the game now is back in the hazard, as the tennis players say.'

Although New Zealand achieved a fourth-innings total which had only once previously been beaten in a Test Match, their 440 left them that tantalising 39 runs short.

E. W. Swanton wrote in the *Daily Telegraph*: 'It would have been poetic justice if the gallant stand by Congdon and Pollard had led to New Zealand's first win over England', while John Arlott in *The Guardian* said: 'Never before in Test cricket have one of the lesser powers forced their way up from humiliation to so close a sight of a win against a major country.'

Congdon went on to score 175 in the next Test. Along with his 176 at Trent Bridge, it was a moment not missed through the sleepless hours as the trace of a tear matched the lump in the throat of a young man listening back home in New Zealand.

Those who heard it will for ever savour the memory created by such stirring, inspirational deeds.

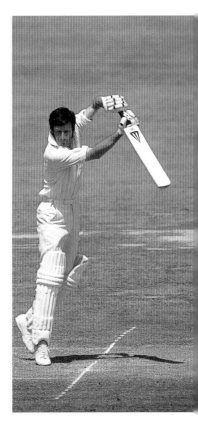

A long hot West Indian summer

In the heatwave of '76, it was England's cricketers who got grilled.
Viv Richards' 291, Michael Holding's 14 for 149, Tony Greig forced to grovel.
Mike Selvey remembers it all too well

ENGLAND v WEST INDIES

THE OVAL, 12-17 AUGUST 1976

W. Indies 687-8 dec	*I. V. A. Richards 291, C. H. Lloyd 84,*
	R. C. Fredericks 71, L. G. Rowe 70,
	C. L. King 63
England 435	*D. L. Amiss 203, A. P. E. Knott 50;*
	M. A. Holding 8-92
W. Indies 182-0 dec	*R. C. Fredericks 86*, C. G. Greenidge 85**
England 203	*A. P. E. Knott 57; M. A. Holding 6-57*
W. Indies won by 231 runs	*(W. Indies won the series 3-0)*

I have this overpowering image, like a still photograph, of The Oval, sun-scorched outfield as brown and tinder-dry as the Kalahari, perhaps twenty minutes before tea on the second day. On a pitch so heartbreakingly flat and easy-paced that Michael Holding's 14 wickets must rate as the greatest piece of sustained fast bowling in history, and with the entire playing area to defend, England were being hammered senseless. And there, standing at the end of his run from the Pavilion End, was Deadly Derek Underwood, face lobstered with the sun and exertion, shirt crumpled and stained with dust, looking forlornly around. Underwood was about to begin his 55th over of the innings; the scoreboard, running hot, read 587 for five.

Two nights previously, at the pre-match dinner, Tony Greig, the England captain, had been rallying

Tony Greig had vowed to make the West Indies grovel. But Michael Holding had other ideas

Scenes from a humiliation

TREVOR BAILEY: *'Seeing Fred come into the box, Brian, I wonder how many times Fred played in a Test Match when the score was 350 on the first day and he'd only bowled nine overs?'*

BRIAN JOHNSTON: *'Yes, it'd be interesting. Anyhow at the moment we're going to see if Richards can get his 200. He's 199. The bowler is going to be Greig bowling from the Vauxhall End. Three men on the off side and in he comes now. Will this be it? The field coming in to save the single and he clips this one away and that is it. It goes to square leg. He's made 200 and I'm afraid there's an invasion of the pitch from all round. This is a tremendous pity. They were asked not to and poor Richards is being mobbed.'*

BILL FRINDALL: *'It's his second double century of the series.'*

TREVOR BAILEY: *'Three hundred up and one feels that England must have a splendid chance of saving this match.'*

TONY COZIER: *'So it's Holding who will continue. The sun streaming across the ground, shadows of the players long, as Lloyd, perhaps the longest of the lot, comes back to his position at fourth slip having given instructions to Holding.*

'Holding now starting to Greig. Greig is 12. 303 for four. Holding's first ball to Greig. He's bowled him! Greig is bowled, right through him, hitting across the yorker and Greig is bowled. A partial invasion of the ground by some West Indian supporters as Greig is bowled by Holding for 12.

'England are 303 for five and they're coming on to the ground, West Indian supporters, more and more now.

They're coming across the pitch as well. Umpire Bird is trying to keep them off. The West Indian players beseeching them not to walk across the pitch. Well, it's fruitless really. Across the ground they're mobbing Holding now. They're lifting him up. Umpire Bird has gone down on his hands and knees.'

JOHN ARLOTT: *'And Holding bowls to him and Amiss plays that past Greenidge again for four runs and now he's actually scored two-thirds of England's runs from the bat – 203 out of 336 for six. And cheerful applause from the West Indians. I suppose that ought to convince anybody that he has conquered this problem.'* [He had been hit on the head by Holding earlier in the season.]

TONY COZIER: *'Willis back to his mark. Phenomenal field to look at when you divert your attention from the middle of the pitch and look to the fielders all over the place. Greenidge goes to deflect this ball down to fine leg, gets too far across, misses the shot. The end of the over. Declaration. The declaration has come with the West Indies 182 for no wicket, 85 to Greenidge, 86 to Fredericks.*

'The West Indies have declared and Tony Greig has gone on his hands and knees and to the delight of the West Indies spectators, now smiling all over his face, gone on his hands and knees and for three or four paces has, in his own words, "grovelled" in front of the West Indian spectators. Well that was a good little touch by Tony Greig and I think the West Indian supporters appreciated it.'

FURTHER EXTRACTS OVERLEAF

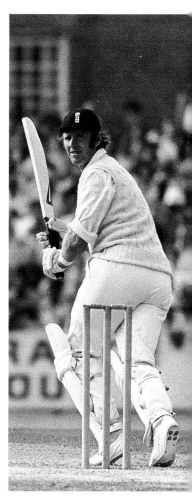

Dennis Amiss returned to the England side with a new batting stance after being hit on the head by Michael Holding earlier in the season. It brought him a double century

Right: Holding bowls Chris Balderstone for nought in the first innings ... and repeated it in the second. Below: Holding celebrates the vital wicket of David Steele

his troops for one last tilt at the tourists who, after draws in the first two Tests, had laid England to waste at Old Trafford, then won a closer encounter at Headingley to take the series. So this was about restoration of pride. Some of Greig's clarion calls were notoriously ill-judged, but now he surpassed himself. Tossing aside the notion that he might make them grovel, he appealed instead for effort.

'Boys,' he said, 'West Indies are a powerful side. They bat hard and they bowl hard. But look at us. We are professionals and this is our stage.' He then drew himself to his full height and surveyed the room, eyes alighting on each man in turn. 'You know,' he concluded, 'we may not be able to bowl like them, and we may not be able to bat like them. But by Christ we can field them off the park.'

Now, although West Indies had Clive Lloyd, Viv Richards and Collis King to patrol the infield (when they needed anything other than a ring of close fielders) and Holding's athleticism on the boundary, the rest in truth were no great shakes. But when Deadly stood back at the end of his run and heaved a sigh, it was hard not to laugh.

Looking around, I recalled Greig's words as I saw to my left in the covers, crouched ready to pounce like panthers, grey-haired David Steele and Peter Willey with his gammy knee, while at mid-off, the other side of a camel called Selvey, Bob Willis lurked. The leg side was little better, guarded by Geoff Miller, Chris Balderstone, a footballer recognised for silky skill rather than pace, wobbly Bob Woolmer and Dennis Amiss, who simply thought fielding was the bloke who wrote *Tom Jones*.

'We can field them off the park.' I looked once more at Underwood, good old faithful Deadly, and my heart bled for him.

Scenes from a humiliation

Left: The wicket the West Indies really wanted was that of Tony Greig, bowled by Michael Holding in both innings. Below: Umpire Dickie Bird has a ringside view of 'Whispering Death' in action

CONTINUED FROM PAGE 73

BRIAN JOHNSTON: *'Holding comes in to Greig, bowls there, and he's bowled him! His leg stump knocked right back plus the middle stump.'*

BILL FRINDALL: *'He is the first West Indies bowler to take 12 wickets in a Test Match against England and only one other bowler, Roberts, has done so in any Test Match for the West Indies.'*

FRED TRUEMAN: *'What a magnificent delivery by Holding. He knows this high backlift of Greig's which they've played on, and he came up the first delivery and bowled the perfect yorker on the leg stump and knocked the leg stump right out of the ground leaving Tony Greig completely nonplussed.'*

JOHN ARLOTT: *'All the West Indian supporters just waiting for this last wicket to fall. To rush on to the field. I'm sure that when it does fall all the players will be trying to beat them to the dressing rooms. In comes Holding. On the way now and hits him on the pad and he's out lbw.*

'The West Indies have won. Willis out lbw to Holding. Holding's sixth wicket in the innings, his 14th in the match.

'Souvenirs have been grabbed. Here come the West Indian supporters swarming over the ground. Selvey is being jostled out in the middle, so are other players and the umpires. Jubilation for the West Indian supporters and the West Indies have won. They've won the series 3-0.'

A stage fit for heroes

*The most famous of all Test Matches. They called it Botham's Ashes,
as he and England came back from the dead to inspire a miraculous series win.
But Messrs Brearley, Dilley and Willis had something to do with it too...*

ENGLAND v AUSTRALIA

HEADINGLEY, 16-21 JULY 1981

● SEE PAGE 81 FOR
THE BEARDED WONDER'S
SOMEWHAT MORE DETAILED
HEADINGLEY '81 SCORECARD

Australia 401	*J. Dyson 102, K. J. Hughes 89;*	
	I. T. Botham 6-95	
England 174	*I. T. Botham 50; D. K. Lillee 4-49*	
England 356	*I. T. Botham 149*; G. R. Dilley 56;*	
	T. M. Alderman 6-135	
Australia 111	*R. G. D. Willis 8-43*	
England won by 18 runs *(England won the series 3-1)*		

The background to perhaps the most remarkable Test Match ever played was extraordinary. England had lost the First Test at Trent Bridge and drawn the Second at Lord's where Ian Botham had, after making a pair of spectacles, resigned from the captaincy a minute or two before he would have been sacked. Mike Brearley, who had given up the captaincy the year before, was resurrected for the Third Test the following week at Headingley

Recalled by Henry Blofeld

and for the rest of the series. He more than anyone at the selection committee meeting later that week would have strongly argued the case for keeping Botham as a player.

For four days the Headingley match unfolded like a nightmare for England, but not so for Botham. Maybe it was Brearley's calming influence which made the difference and created the right atmosphere in the dressing room to help bring back Botham's confidence.

Australia won the toss and an obdurate hundred from opener John Dyson was mainly responsible for taking Australia to 401 for nine declared. From the first ball he bowled, the spring was back in Botham's legs with a vengeance. His six for 95 was the first of his bewildering contributions to the most exciting and dramatic Test Match I shall ever see or commentate about.

The batsmen then made little of Dennis Lillee, Terry Alderman and Geoff Lawson. Botham, who went for his strokes as only he can, was the exception. There were eight spanking fours in his 50 but even Botham was unable to prevent England being bowled out for 174 and being asked to follow on 226 runs behind.

The second time round, Graham Gooch went to Lillee in the first over and at the close of play on the third day England needed another 215 to make Australia bat again.

The next morning, Ladbroke's offered odds of 500/1 against England. When it flashed up on the electronic scoreboard, Lillee and Rod Marsh in the Australian dressing room looked at each other and sent the team coach driver round to the betting tent in the far corner of the ground. It was to become the most famous bet in the history of cricket. But England's batsmen soon made the two Australians feel they had wasted their money.

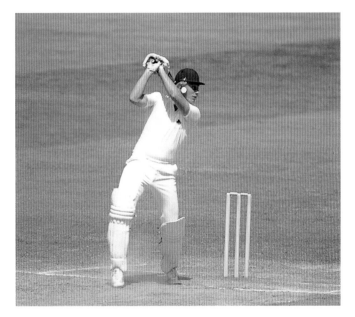

DON MOSEY: *'England now 92 runs away from making Australia bat again as Taylor faces Alderman. He bowls ... and Taylor is caught off bat and pad at short leg, unable to fend off a ball which lifted to the rib area. Taylor is caught Bright, bowled Alderman one, and England are 135 for seven.'*

England were still 91 behind Australia when Botham was joined by Graham Dilley. In the commentary box, Trevor Bailey told us that the writing was on the wall, and half an hour later I said much the same. On the other hand Dilley and Botham – that order is important – had other ideas and, led by Dilley, they put bat to ball most handsomely.

HENRY BLOFELD: *'Although we are in the dying moments of the match, England 170 for seven, still 57 runs behind, we are seeing some attractive cricket. Both Botham, who is 34,*

and Dilley, who is 24, are putting bat to ball and runs are coming at quite a speed and in very entertaining fashion.

HENRY BLOFELD: *Lillee in, bowling now to Botham, outside the off stump ... he hammers this square through the covers. A lovely, forcing shot off the back foot.'*

FRED TRUEMAN: *'Australia have got to bat again.'*

HENRY BLOFELD: *'They have indeed. England are one in the lead.'*

FRED TRUEMAN: *'The Australian bowlers, who have been in command for so long – suddenly, they do not really know where to bowl because the stick is being dished out. They are bowling a bit wide and giving Dilley a lot of room and he is liking that. It is giving him the chance to swing that bat and when he middles it, doesn't it go?'*

Until Botham was joined by Dilley there had been a desperation about his batting which made it look as if it might come to an end at any moment. But Dilley's resolve and splendid strokeplay seemed to inspire his illustrious partner.

Dilley's fifty came when he carved Lillee through the covers off the back foot with power and panache that Botham could only have envied. England were then 243 for seven, only 17 runs ahead and still on the edge of the precipice.

When Dilley was bowled by Alderman for 56, he and Botham had put on 117 for the eighth wicket in 80 minutes but the lead was just 25.

Chris Old took his place and, with a mixture of the improbable and the implausible as well as some fine strokes, helped Botham add another 67 for the ninth

● BILL FRINDALL'S SCORECARD FOR THIS THRILLING PASSAGE OF PLAY IS SHOWN ON PAGE **81**

The most unlikely of all the Headingley heroes was Graham Dilley. The fast bowler was not renowned as a batsman, but it was his swashbuckling devil-may-care approach that inspired Ian Botham's astonishing assault

Geoff Lawson looks on in disbelief as Ian Botham finds ever more outrageous ways to score boundaries on his way to a century off only 87 balls

wicket against an attack which was looking bemused and a captain, Kim Hughes, who was looking bewildered. Botham's hundred came from 87 balls.

ALAN MCGILVRAY: *'Can he get this one run? It's Lawson running in and bowling to him, Botham swings it, it is four runs, it is four more and it's his hundred!'*

TREVOR BAILEY: *'Well, it was a magnificent century. It came quickly, it came in most spectacular fashion. It contained some wonderful shots. We shan't see a better hundred this season.'*

The Australian morale had gone and they were letting the game drift. Old was ninth out at 319 — but still that was not the end of England because Bob Willis now hung around in his own elongated way while Botham threw his bat at everything. They managed to add 37 crucial runs before Willis departed early on the last morning. With Botham left high and dry on 149 not out, Australia still needed only 130 to win.

By then, the psychological advantage had swung completely over to England. Inevitably, Australia's first wicket fell to Botham, who had Graeme Wood caught behind (13 for one). In the meantime, Willis had been bounding up the hill from the Football Ground end as fast as his legs could carry him but without the all-important rhythm. He now asked Brearley to switch him to the Kirkstall Lane end.

Suddenly the rhythm was there to give his bowling the impetus it had previously lacked and he soon had Trevor Chappell caught behind off a nasty lifter (56 for two). But it still seemed straightforward for Australia...

HENRY BLOFELD: *'Willis is bowling the first ball of the over from the Kirkstall Lane end. Up now, he bowls to Hughes. Hughes goes back – he is out! He is caught! He is caught by Botham at third slip, low to his left, and Australia have lost their third wicket for 58. Hughes is out for a duck, caught Botham bowled Willis for nought, and that is the wicket England badly wanted just before lunch...*

'Fifty-eight for three, Australia needing 130 to win. They want 72 more runs and this game is by no means over. A tight attacking field, and here is Willis again, bowling for his life, bowls now to Yallop, bowls and ... he is out! He is caught at forward short leg – he is caught by Gatting. It lifted on him, he played it, could not keep it down, Gatting came forward, got both hands to it, threw it in the air and Australia go in to lunch 58 for four. Yallop caught Gatting bowled Willis for nought. Well, Fred, what an over!'

FRED TRUEMAN: *'What an over, what a transformation!'*

Willis was bowling like a man possessed. Soon after lunch, he had Dyson caught behind (65 for five) and England knew they had a chance, but could they really believe it? That chance was better still when, three runs later, Allan Border was bowled by Old (68 for six). Australia needed 62 more and incredibly it looked as if England were about to pull off the most extraordinary Test match victory of all time.

At 74, Willis charged in again to bowl to Marsh. The ball was short, Marsh hooked and Dilley, as calm as anything, stood his ground with his heels about an inch and a half inside the boundary at fine leg and held the catch in front of his chest (74 for seven). One run later,

Lawson pushed at Willis and Bob Taylor took the catch like a leaping salmon (75 for eight).

It looked all over but now Lillee joined Bright and managed to make batting seem relatively easy. Slowly, runs began to come, in ones and twos and with the odd boundary. The 100 arrived and suddenly after all that had happened it looked as if Australia were going to win after all. One could feel the enthusiasm draining away from the crowd and probably the only entirely composed man on the ground was Mike Brearley. He never showed the slightest sign of panic and was in almost studied control in the slips.

A lovely square cut by Lillee off Willis took Australia to 110 for eight and they needed just 20 more. Willis roared in again, all arms and legs and feverish effort and tousled hair, and Lillee half pulled the ball towards mid-on. Gatting raced in and somehow held on as he fell forwards, taking the catch close to the ground.

I was fortunate enough to be on the air at the time and I shall never forget the sheer excitement and almost unbearable tension as an extra was scampered after Alderman had joined Bright.

TREVOR BAILEY: *'Most of the Australian side inside the dressing room cannot watch.'*

HENRY BLOFELD: *'Willis to Bright, Bright is 19, Australia 111 for nine, 19 short of victory. Here is Willis, in, bowls to Bright ... Bright bowled! The middle stump is out of the ground, England have won! They have won by 18 runs! Willis runs around punching the air, the boys invade the ground and the players run helter-skelter for the pavilion. Well, what a finish. Bright bowled Willis for 19, Willis has taken eight wickets for 43 – the best ever by an English bowler here at Headingley against Australia, a phenomenal performance by Bob Willis and Australia all out for 111. England have won by 18 runs.'*

When Bright's middle stump went cartwheeling, cars hooted their horns vigorously up and down the motorways, high streets, by-roads and lanes of England as drivers heard the news. And presumably Lillee and Marsh will have bought the rest of the Australians drinks that evening.

Ian Botham kept England alive with six first-innings wickets – and Bob Willis finished the Aussies off

The Bearded Wonder's Headingley '81 Scorecard

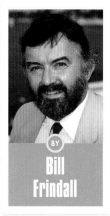

BY
Bill Frindall

Man at work: Bill Frindall composing cryptic entries such as '50 p'ship: 41' and '100 p'ship: 70'

SCORING CHART

```
        5
   6         4
      Bowler
        ▥
7                3
      Batsman
        ▥
   8         2
      9   1
```

Field symbols for right-handed batsman
(reversed for left-handers)

he scorecard opposite is from England's second innings at Headingley in 1981. The page begins with Boycott facing Lillee's last over before lunch on the fourth day; the score is 76 for four. By the end of the page, Botham and Dilley are batting: Botham has 76 and Dilley 47, and the total is 239 for seven. One over before that, I have noted: 'Innings defeat averted'– or, as Fred put it: 'Australia have got to bat again.'

My linear method of scoring is based on that devised by Australia's scorer Bill Ferguson in 1905. It is possible to reconstruct a match ball by ball and to tell exactly what happened to each delivery; who bowled it to whom, from which end, at what time, how the batsman reacted and who was umpiring at each end.

Unless a wicket falls, each line across the various columns contains a full record of one over. The time at which the bowler began his run to deliver the first ball is recorded in the first column (TIME). The bowlers' columns are divided into the two ends of the ground, and the bowler's name and the number of his over in that innings are entered in the appropriate spaces. Each ball is recorded in the columns of the batsman facing it.

At the end of each over all the cumulative total columns are updated (or left blank if they have not changed). These are the six columns on the extreme right of the sheet, and the number of balls faced and boundaries hit by both players in the batting sections.

If a wicket falls, the four columns for the dismissed batsman are ruled off and the rest of the over is recorded two lines below to allow for the incoming batsman's name to be entered.

The NOTES column is used for detailing extras and recording times for partnerships and individual scores when they reach multiples of 50. I also note outstanding fielding, dropped catches, unsuccessful appeals, injuries and other data which may be required to satisfy commentators' enquiries later in the match.

I keep a running total of maidens (M 13) and no-balls (NB /5)

to cross-check my bowling figures and number of balls faced. No-balls are included, as they can be scored off, but wides are ignored, as they cannot. If a batsman is left-handed I write 'LHB' by his name.

I also employ a cryptic method to chart the scoring strokes of each individual innings. It is based on the key shown in the left-hand column of this page. The key is reversed for left-handed batsmen. Though this method is only approximate, it does show if a player has a favourite scoring area or if a bowler tends to concede runs to a particular stroke. It is also possible to reconstruct a scoring chart of a batsman's innings. To make the symbols more exact, I annotate 3/4 above a shot which bisects those two areas (cover and extra cover), and so on. Straightish on-drives are represented by 5/6 and a straight drive which passes the bowler's stumps on the leg side is shown as 5(6).

In 1981, when this scoresheet was done, I also used these symbols when a batsman's intended scoring strokes were fielded and no runs accrued, balls played defensively being shown by a dot above the normal dot. (I now employ the double dot to denote all hits which fail to produce a run, reserving the numbered symbols for scoring strokes; balls ignored by the batsman have no symbol above their dot.) Other symbols which I use are:

B	Bye	P	Hit on pad (no appeal)
E	Edged stroke	S	Sharp (quick) run
EP	Edged ball into pads	X	Played and missed
F	Full toss	Y	Yorker
G	Hit on glove	↑	Bouncer
L	LBW appeal	↓	Shooter
LB	Leg bye	⌒	Bowler used shortened run-up

No-balls (⊙ or ④, etc) and wides (+ or ⊹ etc) are recorded in the conventional way.

HAM'S 149 NOT OUT AT HEADINGLEY

KIRKSTALL LANE END

MAIN STAND END

Minutes	6s	4s
110		8
155		19
219	1	27

Runs	6s	4s
68	1	11
15		3
44		8
22		5

BOTHAM'S SCORING SEQUENCE
000204200004010000100041000031
0013014204*001000404000004040400
44410400000640100040400010201
0001000100010040001000401042041000
40100044100040000000.

* 4 overthrows to the mid-wicket boundary
† off a no-ball

ENGLAND v AUSTRALIA 1981 (3RD TEST) 1981

ENGLAND 2ND INNINGS

(handwritten ball-by-ball scorecard by Bill Frindall)

CRICKET SCORING SHEET No. 1

Designed and drawn by BILL FRINDALL

The Frindall scorecard. Far left: Brian Johnston, Alan McGilvray, and Bill Frindall in fancy dress. 'If we ignore him maybe he'll go away'

A shock from the new kids on the block

*England thought they were doing Sri Lanka a favour by tagging a
one-match 'series' on to the end of their Indian expedition.
But Sri Lanka's first ever Test Match showed they were a team of surprises*

SRI LANKA v ENGLAND

COLOMBO, 17-21 FEBRUARY 1982

Sri Lanka 218	R. S. Madugalle 65, A. Ranatunga 54;
	D. L. Underwood 5-28
England 223	D. I. Gower 89; A. L. F. De Mel 4-70
Sri Lanka 175	R. T. Dias 77; J. E. Emburey 6-33
England 171-3	C. J. Tavaré 85

England won by 7 wickets *(One-match series)*

February 1982. England were in Sri Lanka after an exceptionally tedious six-match series in India, which they had lost one-nil. England teams had been here before, but this was different. Since Sri Lanka's recent elevation to full membership of the International Cricket Conference, they were now a Test-playing country and at the P. Saravanumuttu Stadium (happily for us, more commonly called the Colombo Oval), they would make their debut on this most elevated stage of cricket.

Sri Lanka won the toss, Willis and Botham made early inroads and then Derek Underwood finished them off with five for 28. They were all out for 218 and things were going to the expected plan.

Before lunch on the second day, though, the lively medium pace of Asantha De Mel had plucked out the top three of England's batting with only 40 on the board. David Gower and his captain, Keith Fletcher, retrieved

Eighteen-year-old Arjuna
Ranatunga hit a fine 54...

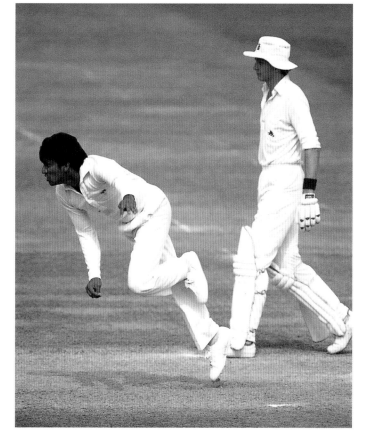

Recalled by Peter Baxter

...then Asantha De Mel shocked a complacent
England by reducing them to 40 for three

the situation to the extent that 200 came up with only five wickets down, but the leg spin of D. S. De Silva provoked another collapse to 223 all out – a lead of just five runs.

By the end of that third day, Sri Lanka made that slender lead entirely superfluous, by losing only three second-innings wickets. At 152 for three they were 147 ahead with plenty of time to go. It was already likely that England would have to bat a great deal better in their second innings to avoid defeat by Test cricket's newest recruits at their first opportunity. Alarm bells were beginning to sound.

Word came later from the dressing room that it was England's vice-captain, Bob Willis, who delivered the harangue that turned his team from the brink of dire embarrassment. The change was certainly dramatic. On the fourth morning, Sri Lanka's last seven wickets fell in the space of three-quarters of an hour for the addition of just eight runs. John Emburey had probably his finest hour with a spell of five for five – six for 33 overall.

England needed 171 to win and, to judge from the way they went about it, were very keen to finish the job on the fourth day – not least, with a flight home the following night, to buy themselves a day off. Chris Tavaré took them to the brink of victory.

DON MOSEY: *'The crowd relatively hushed. Ajit De Silva, left-arm slow bowler. And Tavaré is beaten by this – beaten in the air – and he's out! He's bowled ... stumped! He played over the top of it. I saw the bails dislodged and wasn't sure for a minute, but the official verdict is: Tavaré, with 85 runs to his credit, stumped Goonatillake, bowled Ajit*

De Silva. And England, needing four to win, lose the man who has steered them so close to victory. It's 167 for three.

'So it's Gower, who has got 38 runs behind him, facing De Mel. There's certainly no more than one over after this, if that, to be bowled in the day. De Mel in. Gower drives through the covers. A magnificent shot to end the game. Turns and stalks away to the pavilion. That is accomplishing victory in the grand manner.

'A magnificent shot to finish the historic inaugural Test Match in Sri Lanka. England have won by seven wickets, with Gower not out 42. It's accomplished with five minutes of the fourth day to spare.

'Experience and class told in the end, but there's clearly a bright future for Sri Lankan cricket.'

What we did not know at the time, but found out soon after, was that Messrs Gooch, Emburey and Underwood from that team would be taking an almost immediate flight to South Africa and the first 'rebel' tour. For Derek Underwood, who had taken eight wickets in that Test to take him to 289 overall, it was particularly poignant, for he never played for England again.

Ranjan Madugalle's fighting 65 rescued Sri Lanka's first innings, and D. S. De Silva's leg breaks so nearly left England red-faced

The one that nearly got away

Geoff Miller's juggling act sealed the closest victory in Test Match history.
His England team-mate Graeme Fowler remembers it well
– he was cheering from a Melbourne hotel sick bed

AUSTRALIA v ENGLAND

MELBOURNE, 26-30 DECEMBER 1982

England 284	C. J. Tavaré 89, A. J. Lamb 83
Australia 287	K. C. Wessels 162; R. G. D. Willis 5-66
England 294	G. Fowler 65; J. R. Thomson 5-73
Australia 288	D. W. Hookes 68, A. R. Border 62*;
	N. G. Cowans 6-77

England won by 3 runs *(Australia won the series 2-1)*

Australia, nine wickets down, needed four runs for victory. Ian Botham bowled a short ball that swung away from Jeff Thomson, he followed it and it flew off the edge of his bat straight to Chris Tavaré at second slip. The ball bounced tantalisingly out of his hands and over his shoulder – but Geoff Miller at first slip ran behind Tavaré and completed the catch. It was the narrowest victory ever in Test cricket.

Norman Cowans set up the final drama when he took his sixth wicket in the innings…

PAUL SHEAHAN: *'Eight for 218 and Australia struggling now as Hogg faces the hero of this innings, Norman Cowans … and he's hit on the pads. And it's out! He's been given out, lbw. The ball struck the front pad of Hogg, but Hogg only played six inches or so in front of the crease and there's no doubt in my mind the ball would have hit the stumps.'*

Recalled by Graeme Fowler

Jeff Thomson took five wickets in all, but it was his batting that nearly won it for Australia

Australia were still 73 runs behind when Jeff Thomson walked out to join Allan Border. But Border farmed the strike in a typically obstinate last-wicket stand which took them to the brink of victory…

HENRY BLOFELD: *'Ian Botham is going to have one last crack at Jeff Thomson. 288 for nine, four to win for Australia, three to tie, Thomson has 21 and Border has 62. And Botham now bowls to Thomson. Thomson plays. He drops it … and he's out! He's caught in the slips! Tavaré knocked it up and it was Miller who caught the rebound.*

'England have won by three runs and the England fielders are running off the ground, snatching the stumps. Poor Thomson and Border walk back utterly dejected. England have won by three runs, equalling the lowest margin of victory. What an astonishing end to the match.'

Although I was playing in the match, I witnessed the victory on my hotel room television. Jeff Thomson had broken my big toe in three places with a yorker. To this day the bone is still in three pieces. Having passed fifty for the second time in the series – but the first time with confidence – that yorker ended my tour.

I wasn't the only batsman to have tough luck at Melbourne. Greg Chappell took guard against Norman Cowans to receive his first ball. Allan Lamb, stationed at deep square, was 120 yards from the wicket. Cowans, young and very fast, bowled Chappell a bouncer. With superb balance, timing and power, Chappell hooked the ball like a tracer bullet. Lamb ran 25 yards and took a superb catch. In 17 years of professional cricket, not once did I hit a ball as well as the one that caused Chappell's dismissal.

Of the match itself I only recall odd incidents: Allan Border used Ian Botham's bat. Ian Gould, who fielded for us, took a fantastic catch. Sixty-four thousand people watched the first day. But two things I will never forget: Geoff Miller's catch, and the look of relief on Chris Tavaré's face.

Geoff Miller's bowling accounted for Jeff Thomson in the first innings – but it was his catch to take Thommo's wicket in the second innings that sealed the match, leaving Allan Border (left) high and dry

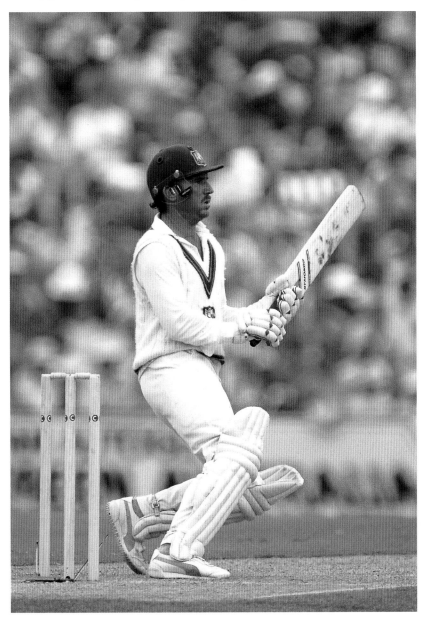

Greenidge makes light work of it

When David Gower waited until well into the final morning to declare,
341 runs ahead, he was accused of being over-cautious.
But when Gordon Greenidge was around, no target was safe...

Gordon Greenidge and
Larry Gomes made a
target of 342 look easy.
Ian Botham (right) took
eight for 103 in West
Indies' first innings – but
0 for 117 in the second

ENGLAND v WEST INDIES

LORD'S, 28 JUNE-3 JULY 1984

England 286	*G. Fowler 106, B. C. Broad 55;*
	M. D. Marshall 6-85
West Indies 245	*I. V. A. Richards 72; I. T. Botham 8-103*
England 300-9 dec	*A. J. Lamb 110, I. T. Botham 81*
West Indies 344-1	*C. G. Greenidge 214*, H. A. Gomes 92**
West Indies won by 9 wickets	*(West Indies won the series 5-0)*

It was a bit of bluster designed to stir up the affable host at lunch on the final day of the 1984 Test at Lord's. Alec Dibbs, the larger-than-life President of MCC at the time, had invited me to his box over the old Tavern in company with a few West Indian High Commissioners and other dignatories, and the interval had arrived with the West Indies 82 for one after David Gower's delayed declaration half an hour into the day had challenged them to get 342 to win.

'We'll get these in a canter,' I proclaimed. It got the conversation going all right, but even optimistic West Indians such as Algy Symmonds, with whom I had shared many commentaries in Barbados and who was now High Commissioner in London, took it with a pinch of salt — and another mouthful of smoked salmon. President Dibbs simply chuckled politely.

After all, up to this point England had supplied the stars of the match

— Graeme Fowler and Allan Lamb had scored centuries, while Ian Botham had trumped Malcolm Marshall's six-wicket haul in England's first innings by taking eight.

BRIAN JOHNSTON: *'Botham is running from the Nursery End now to bowl to Garner, and he's nicked it. He's caught, again well in front of first slip, by Downton, a good falling catch. Garner caught Downton bowled Botham for six. West Indies are all out for 245 and that means that Botham has got his eight wickets and now needs five to take 300. Milton Small is not out three, which will improve his batting average in his career.*

'And naturally enough Botham is going to be shoved forward by the side to take the cheers from the crowd, who are standing to him. You don't often see people taking eight wickets. Botham being very modest, but Gower waiting and letting Botham lead the side in. England lead by 41.'

Yet my remark to Alec Dibbs wasn't all braggadoccio. Gordon Greenidge was batting and had already belted ten fours in 54. When he was in the mood there was

Recalled by Tony Cozier

no more devastating batsman in the game – and he was on song here. And although Desmond Haynes was run out at 57 (the first time in seven Tests the West Indies had lost a second-innings wicket), the phlegmatic left-hander Larry Gomes was Greenidge's partner and Viv Richards, Clive Lloyd and Jeffrey Dujon were to follow.

By the time I thanked Alec Dibbs for his hospitality and hurried off to the TMS box, there were worried looks on the few English faces round the table. Gomes had been dropped at slip by Derek Pringle off Neil Foster when five and Greenidge had been caught off a Bob Willis no-ball at 29 and put down at cover by Graeme Fowler, of all fielders, off Foster, at 83. The force was obviously with the West Indies.

BRIAN JOHNSTON: *'Willis is running in, his feet in exactly the same places as he comes in now. Bowls to Greenidge on 99. Greenidge cuts this one and this is going to be it. It goes to Fowler, but he is deeper this time. Greenidge gets his 100. The bat in the air. He takes his cap off. No one, thank goodness, has run on to congratulate him. But we all applaud him from here and so do the crowd. A very fine 100. The West Indies are 149 for one.'*

TREVOR BAILEY: *'Yes, it was a splendid hundred, but we have*

now seen Willis bowling. That over only conceded two runs and if he goes on bowling like that it's going to make life extremely difficult, because Willis is not easy to hit with a defensive field – which he has got now.'

Gower's defence was in vain. Between lunch and tea, Greenidge simply stood up and dispatched the ball to all parts while Gomes gathered his runs more with timing and placement than power. In 25 overs in the two hours, another 17 boundaries were struck and 132 added. The target was only 128 away at the start of the last session and the two West Indians were unstoppable. By the time David Evans and Barry Meyer, the umpires, signalled the mandatory final 20 overs, there was the formality of scoring another 43. Only 8.1 overs were required.

Greenidge passed the first of his four Test double-hundreds with a hooked six off Foster and walked off in the evening sunshine unbeaten on 214 with another six and 29 fours. Gomes, the ideal foil, was 92 and the champagne was being popped in the dressing room – and, I believe, in the MCC President's Box as well – even as the winning run was struck to complete what was an astonishing, if not entirely surprising, victory.

TONY COZIER: *'Gordon Greenidge has set up this victory with an innings of 214 in which he has hammered the ball all over the ground with complete assurance and confidence. Larry Gomes, the left-hander, less powerful but no less effective, is 87.*

'Ian Botham is going to bowl this over. He's going to bowl spin. Downton is up to the stumps. The West Indies need two more to win and let's see what he does. Ian Botham off two or three paces is bowling from the Pavilion End and he comes in now to Gomes and Gomes goes back and hits the winning runs through the off side for four. The West Indies have won this match by nine wickets, 344 for one, having been set 342 to win.

'Gordon Greenidge finishes 214 not out. Larry Gomes is 92 not out. The West Indies go two-nil up in the series with one of the most remarkable victories in the history of Test cricket. The crowd is swarming on to the ground. The West Indies have won the match with eleven overs to go.'

Mike Gatting takes cover as Gomes hits out – but the real destroyer of England's hopes was Gordon Greenidge (left)

Mr Cool loses his rag

Suave, sophisticated, elegant … David Gower was all these things.
But a rabble-rouser? Just once. Vic Marks was among a select audience
who saw Gower play Henry V in India. And it worked

Henry V Part II: After his
up-and-at-'em speech,
David Gower's team won
the series. Tim Robinson
(right) pitched in with 160

INDIA v ENGLAND

DELHI, 12-17 DECEMBER 1984

India 307	*Kapil Dev 60; R. M. Ellison 4-66*
England 418	*R. T. Robinson 160, P. R. Downton 74,*
	A. J. Lamb 52; Shivaramakrishnan 6-99
India 235	*S. M. Gavaskar 65, M. Amarnath 64;*
	P. H. Edmonds 4-60, P. I. Pocock 4-93
England 127-2	

***England won by 8 wickets** (England won the series 2-1)*

The Delhi Test of 1984 was memorable for a number of reasons – the least of which was that I made my first appearance on TEST MATCH SPECIAL, though still a player. It was the second Test of the series but already it had been a momentous tour. Twenty-four hours after the England team arrived, India's Prime Minister, Mrs Gandhi, had been assassinated. Twenty-four hours before the First Test in Bombay the British Deputy High Commissioner, Percy Norris, had also been assassinated. We all assumed we would be going home.

Instead, the Bombay Test was played. England lost, and it was then feared that the series might mirror the tortuous path of Keith Fletcher's tour four years earlier – an Indian victory followed by four drab draws.

But at Delhi we were surprised. The pitch, grassless of course, presented a mosaic of cracks, and

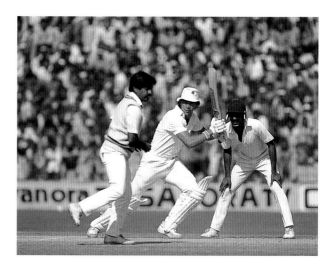

around them the soil was ominously loose. India's captain, Sunil Gavaskar, suggested we should all arrange a visit to the Taj Mahal for the fifth day. But, defying the pundits, the pitch refused to deteriorate. Indeed by lunch on the final day the match seemed destined to be drawn.

England had procured a first-innings lead of 111 thanks to a superb 160 from Tim Robinson.

TONY LEWIS: *'Every possible tension for young Tim Robinson under that white sun hat. Again looks down the pitch at Shivaramakrishnan, who comes in now. A chopped shot by Robinson, Shastri fields, throws, Downton's in! And Robinson has*

Recalled by Vic Marks

his maiden Test century with a delicate dab square on the off side. His hat falls off as he runs. He's now hatless. Congratulations from the Indian players, who pass him and put a hand on his back. Paul Downton is shaking his hand and no doubt renewing the pledge that they must bat together to get England up to India's score. So it's 247 for five. And Tim Robinson has reached the magic three figures, 100 not out.'

But by lunch on the fifth day India were 204 for four, a lead of 95. At the interval the English dressing room was angry at a few umpiring decisions and there was more resignation than optimisim in the air. Captain Gower then stunned his team-mates by deserting his laid-back image and haranguing his men in most un-Gower-like terms. The message, suitably diluted, was: 'Do you want to win this Test or not?'

Something clicked. After lunch India collapsed spectacularly to England's spinners, Edmonds and Pocock. Not that I witnessed the drama. I was dutifully wheeling away in the nets to Bruce French under the instructions of coach Norman Gifford. The pitch was out of sight, but we could see the scoreboard. When four wickets had fallen in 20 minutes, even the indefatigable Gifford was persuaded that net practice might be abandoned.

Kapil Dev, we learnt, had been at his irresponsible worst, out slogging – which so annoyed his captain that India's megastar was dropped for the next Test.

TONY LEWIS: *'Pocock is in to Kapil Dev. Down the pitch – it's a lofted six! It's a handsome stroke over long on, and that cleared the boundary by some 20, 30 yards. Six more runs, 214 for five India. Kapil Dev now seven.*

'Pocock comes in, tries again. Again floated up, up in the air – it's a miscue. He's caught! Lamb has caught him! Well bowled by Pocock, who floated the ball very carefully indeed. Kapil could not resist it. His eyes went round in

his head, he took a tremendous swipe for a huge six. Lamb had to back-pedal at mid-off and in the end caught an excellent catch, two-handed at chest high. So that's Kapil Dev rather dramatically disappearing, caught Lamb bowled Pocock for seven, and India are 214 now for six.'

ABBAS ALI BAIG: *'A very irresponsible shot that Kapil played that time. Having hit the previous ball for a very well-*

timed six, he repeated the shot. I think very clever bowling on the part of Pocock. He held this one back a bit and threw it up and pitched it a little outside the off stump, inviting Kapil to drive, and Kapil fell for the trap.'

Suddenly England needed just 125 in slightly under two hours for a rare overseas victory.

Now Peter Baxter appeared, looking a little more perplexed than usual. He was frantically searching for a stray Englishman, *any* stray Englishman, since his summariser, Mike Selvey, had suddenly been laid low with stomach cramps, as sometimes happens in Delhi. I gladly volunteered, and watched Gatting and Lamb knock off the runs from the radio box in the company of Tony Lewis, who had overseen England's win in Delhi in 1972.

Still stunned by the ease of our victory, we celebrated – in those pre-Veuve Clicquot days – with sausage, egg and chips and cans of John Smith's bitter in the bar of the British High Commission.

India's captain Sunil Gavaskar led their second-innings resistance. But Gower's lunchtime lecture gave Gavaskar food for thought

Gooch joins the immortals

There has never been a match like it. Gooch wrote his name in cricket's history books
with a titanic triple Nelson. But when it came to saving the follow-on,
it was Kapil Dev who turned a blind eye to convention

ENGLAND v INDIA

LORD'S, 26-31 JULY 1990

England 653-4 dec	*G. A. Gooch 333, A. J. Lamb 139,*
	*R. A. Smith 100**
India 454	*M. Azharuddin 121, R. J. Shastri 100,*
	Kapil Dev 77, D. B. Vengsarkar 52;*
	A. R. C. Fraser 5-104
England 272-4 dec	*G. A. Gooch 123, M. A. Atherton 72*
India 224	

England won by 247 runs *(England won the series 1-0)*

O f the great experiences of any cricket enthusiast's life, the games at Lord's tend to stand out. The mind's eye sees that magnificent ground in retrospect forever bathed in a golden sunshine. In the case of the 1990 Test Match between England and India, memory does not lie. It was hot; it was sunny; the air was full of excitement and good cheer; and the events of the match unfolded as if in celebration of the game itself.

The match aggregate of 1,603 runs eclipsed by two the classic Lord's Test of 1930 when Donald Bradman played what he believes to have been his best innings (254 before being brilliantly caught by Percy Chapman) and Chapman and Bill Woodfull became the first Anglo-Australian captains to make centuries in the same Test. There was another echo of that

Recalled by Christopher Martin-Jenkins

game in 1990, because Graham Gooch and Mohammed Azharuddin each played his most famous innings.

For Gooch it was the game which ensured immortality. He scored 333 and 123, led England to their second successive Test win (a feat last achieved five years earlier) and ended the match with a deadly throw from mid-on to enable England to win by 247 runs. It sounds one-sided, but it was not. India responded to England's 653, after Azharuddin had foolishly put them in, by making 454 and they were 114 for three at noon on the last day, still with a realistic chance of a draw and romantic dreams, at least, of chasing 472 to win. On such a true pitch, why not?

Angus Fraser's accuracy was as good a reason as any.

Right: Graham Gooch and Allan Lamb take a breather on the way to 333 and 139 respectively

He took eight for 143 in the match, a performance perhaps most fairly compared to Kapil Dev's one for 173. India's greatest modern all-rounder was not to let such a glittering match go without making his own mark on it, but when his captain wanted him to make quick incisions on the first morning, the best he could manage was to bowl Mike Atherton for eight.

England were 82 for one at lunch and 359 for two at the close of the first day. Gooch had been dropped behind the wicket on 36 but was 194 not out when stumps were drawn and he pounded the Indian bowlers remorselessly for most of Friday too, putting on 308 with Allan Lamb and declaring soon after Manoj Prabhakar had bowled him for 333 off 485 balls. He had hit three sixes and 43 fours and it was the highest score ever made at Lord's.

BRIAN JOHNSTON: *'Gooch is looking round and funnily enough, well not funnily enough, they've brought the long off and the long on in so that he can't pinch the single. Now here's the ball as Shastri runs up, now round the wicket,*

bowls to Gooch, Gooch just tickles that — that's it! He's got his 300. He tickled it down to long leg and Gooch is 300 not out. And the crowd rising to him. Shastri congratulates him, the Indian team applaud. I haven't seen the umpires do so, that's not done, but a marvellous performance and I think the first one on which I have commentated.'*

CHRISTOPHER MARTIN-JENKINS: *'We have connoisseurs here today, clearly, and they're seeing history in the making. They may go home and say, "I was there when Graham Gooch broke the world Test record", but he'll get a big cheer also, I am sure, if he declares when Smith gets his hundred, which must be one possibility. The clock going up to five o'clock. He's got 333 not out as Prabakhar bowls to him — and he's bowled him!*

'Graham Gooch, bowled Prabhakar 333. Almost the world stopped for a second in amazement and then the crowd erupted in congratulations for Prabhakar and still greater congratulations for the England captain, Graham Gooch of Essex, who has succumbed at what some people might think is an unlucky score of 333. He and the crowd

That familiar Gooch sweep and, below, the moment when 'almost the world stopped for a second in amazement'

who saw it will never forget this innings. Off comes his white helmet, up comes his weighty blade, risen to the crowd. And let's just hear the noise as he disappears into the sanctuary of the Pavilion.'

FAROKH ENGINEER: *'Lovely to see the whole England team clapping him all the way to the Pavilion. The non-striker Robin Smith, his bat down, his gloves off, clapping him. I think even Dickie Bird had a few claps and it's fantastic — what a superb innings and the proverbial triple Nelson has done it again, 333.'*

CMJ: *'Done it again? When did you last see it done?'*

Azharuddin could not upstage Graham Gooch for power or stamina, but his century on the Saturday was the finest example of wristy wizardry in this most engaging cricketer's long career. He was scintillating as he drove and cut the ball past cover or flicked it to the mid-wicket boundary like a puck across the ice.

CMJ: *'Fraser from the Nursery End bowls to him and Azharuddin flicks it away towards the mid-wicket boundary, and there is his hundred. As good a hundred as you will ever have seen. Flicked out towards the mid-wicket boundary for three runs, and listen to the reception.'*

FAROKH ENGINEER: *'Absolutely brilliant there. Azharuddin waving his bat to all corners of the ground. One of the finest hundreds I've seen at Lord's. We've seen some great innings from Gooch, Lamb, Smith, but certainly this takes the cake.'*

Everyone was talking about Azhar on Sunday — the day of rest which cricket authorities have abandoned to their everlasting shame — but Eddie Hemmings bowled him for 121 early on Monday and soon India needed 24 to save the follow-on with their last pair together. Kapil's response was extraordinary.

CMJ: *'There's a forward short leg as the only close fielder and a man at fine leg about 15 yards in from the fence. There are four men out towards the leg side boundary, two on the off side and a forward short leg. Up comes Hemmings. He bowls — and this is a big hit. It has gone right over the sight screen for six! And a massive stroke it was. It hit the little bit of tarpaulin that separates the two new stands, and it would have gone halfway into the Nursery ground if that hadn't stopped it. It takes Kapil Dev to 59. The total to 436 for nine. '454 is the magic figure. Hemmings bowls, down the pitch he comes, tries it again, it's going to be another six! Over long on, miles over long on. It was about nine again, not six.'*

TREVOR BAILEY: *'Lovely shot. He doesn't half hit the ball. It's the high back lift, everything there. And now I reckon he wants a single.'*

CMJ: *'Sixty-five to him — what a marvellous bit of batting by Kapil Dev. Hemmings quite rightly giving him the bait. He comes in now and that's a bit flatter. He goes for the hit again. He could be caught. No, it's another six! Three in a row! That was lower and even harder off a ball that was not tossed up. Eighteen off three balls.'*

BILL FRINDALL: *'That's equalled the world record for three successive sixes, the most ever hit. Sylvester Clarke and Walter Hammond — but not in the same match.'*

CMJ: *'This has been one of best mornings' cricket I have ever seen, I think. 448 for nine. Kapil Dev 71 not out. And now India, from being absolutely at the Gates of Doom, so to speak, if you consider the follow-on in cricketing terms potential doom anyway, now they are at the Gates of Paradise, because they need only six more —*

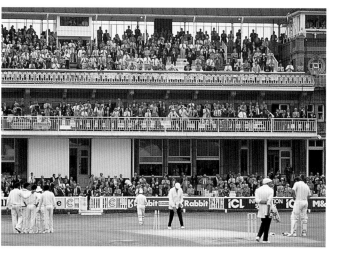

Right: The Lord's Pavilion rises to acclaim Graham Gooch, out for 333

Not exactly the textbook method of saving the follow-on. Kapil Dev strides down the pitch and imperiously smashes Eddie Hemmings for his fourth six in a row

and that can be done in one shot.'

TREVOR BAILEY: *'It's a very difficult one, I can't read Kapil Dev's mind.'*

CMJ: *'One more ball in the over.'*

TREVOR BAILEY: *'My own feeling is to go for the single now.' (Guffaws from back of commentary box.) 'But I think he might go for another biggie.'*

CMJ: *'You didn't often go for four sixes in a row, Trevor. Well, here's the last ball of the over. Hemmings bowls it. Kapil Dev is going for the big hit. It's going to do it, is it? He's done it! He's saved the follow-on. He's broken a world record. He shakes his fist to the Indian dressing room and if that isn't one of the most remarkable things you've ever seen in cricket, I don't know what is. Four sixes in a row just when England seemed to have it all sewn up. Fantastic batting.'*

TREVOR BAILEY: *'I'm speechless. I've never seen that happen before. I don't think I shall ever see it happen again.'*

CMJ: *'He's smiling, as well he might.'*

BILL FRINDALL: *'He's not only beaten the record for the most sixes off consecutive balls, he's equalled the record for the most runs in a six-ball over. That's the fourth instance of 24.'*

TREVOR BAILEY: *'And in that situation!'*

CMJ: *'Incredible. Well, 454 for nine. Fraser bowls to Hirwani. It keeps low. He's lbw! Well, what an extraordinary game is cricket and what a wonderful game this has been. And by one run India have avoided the follow-on.'*

Gooch, confident as a feudal baron among his peasants, clattered his second century of the match to set up the declaration, but it was not until Dilip Vengsarkar was caught behind by Jack Russell off Hemmings, having batted beautifully on his favourite ground, that England could feel at all confident of rewarding their captain.

Return of the exiles

Mike Atherton had dirt in his trousers, but it made no odds to the South Africans.
They took England to the cleaners as the home of cricket
welcomed them back after 29 years

Michael Atherton hit his
lowest point as England
captain, but it could not
mar an historic occasion
as South Africa's openers
strode out at Lord's for
the first time in 29 years

ENGLAND v SOUTH AFRICA

LORD'S, 21-24 JULY 1994

South Africa 357	K. C. Wessels 105, G. Kirsten 72;
	D. Gough 4-76
England 180	A. A. Donald 5-74
S. Africa 278-8 dec	D. Gough 4-46
England 99	
South Africa won by 356 runs *(Series drawn 1-1)*	

South African cricket lovers had already experienced about 25 unforgettable moments and at least a dozen historic days by the time we arrived at Lord's for the first of three Tests in 1994. But however tired the phrases had become, we all knew that this was special.

JONATHAN AGNEW: *'The ground virtually full. People quickly now taking their seats and awaiting the arrival of the South African batsmen. Andrew Hudson, who made a century on his Test debut in Barbados against the West Indies which South Africa eventually lost. And here's the hand now for South Africa's batsmen, and all round the ground people rise to their feet. A tremendous ovation for South Africa's opening batsmen. The first time they've walked out at Lord's for 29 years and what a moment for them.'*

The team had had nets on the Nursery ground before the match, and I was

Recalled by Gerald De Kock

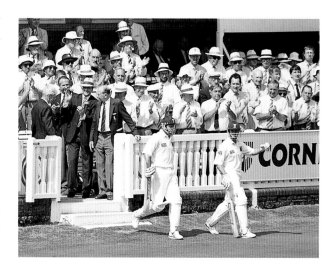

one of several journalists over-robustly shooed away from the hallowed playing surface after peering at it from the playing edge. However, I *was* able to interview the England captain in the car park. It must be Lord's.

Nearly a decade of broadcasting and commentating seemed not to have prepared me for my first day with TMS, and I was almost consumed with nerves on the first morning. The first twenty-minute stint seemed to last three minutes, however, and I was soon being tapped on the shoulder to make way for CMJ. I wasn't the only South African on duty. The trouble was that working with the great Barry Richards, whom I had seeen little of since his emigration to Australia, only heightened my anxiety (and very soon enjoyment).

Despite a goodly scattering of old school and MCC ties, it was not long before I realised that no opinions were ever cast in stone and there really were chocolate cakes in the box (or was it banana muffins?). I soon came to know what I had always believed, that TMS was the ultimate mix of work and fun.

Trevor Bailey finished the Test in plaster after kicking a flower bed and Aggers dealt with the jovial, jacketed and tieless Archbishop Tutu with aplomb.

DESMOND TUTU: *'I used to live in Golders Green and came here in 1963 for the first time. But this is just out of the world for our country, for everybody. The weather is just heaven-made.'*

JONATHAN AGNEW: *'It's certainly been a bonus today, hasn't it? And Gough is no doubt perspiring a little. Dries his hand on the back of his trousers and sets off again from this Pavilion End. Bowls to Peter Kirsten and there's an appeal for a catch. Kirsten is not moving but Dickie Bird is now seeing him on his way. The finger goes up.'*

DESMOND TUTU: *'Oh dear.'*

JONATHAN AGNEW: *'And England have taken their fourth wicket, much to Archbishop Tutu's dismay.'*

DESMOND TUTU: *(Laughing.) 'Oh, how horrible. We were coming to thump you here, man!'*

JONATHAN AGNEW: *'Well, you may still do that. 164 for four is the score. Peter Kirsten on his way.'*

It was of course also an historic Test in the field. Kepler scored a gravelly captain's hundred on the first day and then England, with Darren Gough injured, were bowled out for 99 in 40 overs on day four.

GERALD DE KOCK: *'McMillan bowls to Fraser, back in front of his stumps. He's out! It's all over... Or is it? They're not sure. The South Africans think it is. They've ripped out a stump at this end, De Villiers has. And Fraser is out and Rhodes is on his way, and I don't think Darren Gough is coming out, and England are 99 for nine. Rhodes is jogging back towards the dressing room and the South Africans have won at Lord's in somewhat strange fashion.*

'They've won by 356 runs — an immense victory by a team who've given their all on their first outing at Lord's. Allan Donald has the ball in his hand. High fives from McMillan and Donald. A wonderful moment for all of South Africa.'

BARRY RICHARDS: *'That is a comprehensive victory. At no stage did England really threaten. Once Wessels and Kirsten had established themselves in the second session of the first day, it was all downhill for England from then.*

'It will be a very emotional night inside the South African dressing room tonight. There will be a lot of rejoicing, not just with the players who have done the job, but with a lot of the fans from South Africa that have come to watch — I couldn't help thinking as I walked round the ground that it was almost like being at Newlands, there were so many people.

'And I can see a South African flag down there. I think in the initial stages, Gerald, we weren't sure which way round it went. It's all new for us.'

Even Hansie Cronje joined in the celebrations with Kepler Wessels and Allan Donald as South Africa celebrated their Lord's comeback – and managed to wave the flag the right way up

Mike Procter waved his flag on the balcony in defiance of local authority and Wessels and his (previously sour-faced) lieutenant Hansie Cronje finished the night pouring beer on everyone's heads. Unfettered, uncomplicated cricketing joy.

Some people said the Test would be remembered for another reason, but not me. My TMS debut and South Africa's four-day 356-run win far outweighed whatever the hell it was Mike Atherton had in his pocket.

· OLD TRAFFORD 1995 ·

Cork's triple whammy

Anyone arriving late on Sunday 30 July 1995 missed one of the rarest sights in cricket – a hat-trick. And by the evening there was another rare sight: an England victory against the West Indies

ENGLAND v WEST INDIES

OLD TRAFFORD, 27-30 JULY 1995

W. Indies 216	*B. C. Lara 87; A. R. C. Fraser 4-45, D. G. Cork 4-86*
England 437	*G. P. Thorpe 94, D. G. Cork 56*; C. A. Walsh 4-92*
W. Indies 314	*B. C. Lara 145; D. G. Cork 4-111*
England 94-4	
England won by 6 wickets	*(Series drawn 2-2)*

The fourth Cornhill Test Match in 1995 against the West Indies was played at Old Trafford. England won in four days. That statistic sets the scene. I always felt that coming back to Old Trafford with the TEST MATCH SPECIAL commentary team was so special: it brought back many happy memories for me as a player. With a full house it was a perfect stage for an international player to perform.

On this occasion two truly did. Brian Lara scored a magnificent 145 in West Indies' second innings and one was in awe of his strokeplay. But it was England's Dominic Cork who was Man of the Match, due mainly to his stunning performance in his first over of the fourth day.

In the commentary box I recall we were not actually settled in, not just comfy. Coffee had to be quaffed and there were inevitably a couple of late arrivals.

Recalled by David Lloyd

Traffic y'know. West Indies started the day 62 runs behind with seven wickets in hand and Lara at the crease. But England got the perfect start as Ritchie Richardson rather unfortunately played on to Cork to make it 161 for four.

JONATHAN AGNEW: *'Cork bowls. Oh, and he's played on! In the first over of the day! Trying to leave the ball alone, he got an inside edge on to his stumps. A vital breakthrough for Engand. Ritchie Richardson out, bowled by Dominic Cork for 22. It's a fortunate dismissal – he was trying to take the bat out of the way and he did it slightly too late. The* ball cannoned off the inside edge into the stumps and there's a very disappointed West Indian captain trudging off towards the Pavilion. All the players dashed up to congratulate Dominic Cork, who would have missed the off stump by a foot – and that little bit of rub of the green goes England's way. 161 for four.'

To the new batsman, Junior Murray, fast, full and straight was the order of the day – and Cork did not disappoint.

JONATHAN AGNEW: *'Two runs scored this morning, the West Indies have lost a wicket. Away goes Cork and bowls to Murray, who is hit on the pad. He appeals for leg before wicket and he's out lbw! Cork's on a hat-trick! A*

set, you could hear a pin drop. Hat-trick on – c'mon son, same ball, same place, same result…

JONATHAN AGNEW: *'So Cork on a hat-trick. Three slips, a gully, two men around the bat. Away he goes, bowling to Carl Hooper. He bowls now, Hooper is hit on the pad, there's an appeal…'*

DAVID LLOYD: *'He's out.'*

JONATHAN AGNEW: *'Umpire Mitchley has given him out lbw. Cork has taken a hat-trick in his first over of the day! He's mobbed by his team-mates and he's flung to the ground and Hooper departs now. What a start. There's a standing ovation from this near full house for Dominic Cork, and that surely must put a seal on this match. Carl Hooper, leg*

1. 'Howzat!'
Ritchie Richardson,
bowled Dominic Cork, 22.

2. 'Howzat!!!'
Junior Murray,
lbw Dominic Cork, 0.

3. 'HowZAAAATTT!!!!!!!'
Carl Hooper,
lbw Dominic Cork, 0.

terrible start for the West Indies as they try and save this match. Murray's out first ball, lbw to Dominic Cork, and what a start for England – 161 for five and Murray can barely drag himself off the ground. Leg before, first ball, and I must admit from here that it looked absolutely plum. He shuffled in front of his stumps and got hit bang in front.'

The coffee took a back seat now as Bill Frindall busily looked up 'Hat-tricks'. 'Good start for England' was the call. Now, can he do it?

Cork can get pumped up, but here he was completely focused. The obligatory attacking field was

before, first ball. Umpire Miitchley thought about it for a moment or two, but like Junior Murray he seemed to get right across in front of his stumps and there's an elated-looking Dominic Cork mopping his brow, a hug and a kiss from Angus Fraser, the big fast bowler who came over and shook him by the hand. It's the end of Dominic Cork's first over and he is wandering around, he doesn't know where to go at the moment. He's absolutely on Cloud Nine.'

Cork transformed the game that morning and it was a wonderful achievement. There was great euphoria in the commentary box and with six hours still to go, it set us up for the win that squared the series.

Iron Mike, marathon man

Four wickets down, 344 runs adrift, over a day to go.
Everything was set up for the all too familiar England collapse.
But Michael Atherton and Jack Russell had other ideas

SOUTH AFRICA v ENGLAND

JOHANNESBURG, 30 NOVEMBER-4 DECEMBER 1995

South Africa 332	G. Kirsten 110, D. J. Cullinan 69;
	D. G. Cork 5-84, D. E. Malcolm 4-62
England 200	R. A. Smith 52
S. Africa 346-9 dec	B. M. McMillan 100*, D. J. Cullinan 61;
	D. G. Cork 4-78
England 351-5	M. A. Atherton 185*
Match drawn	(South Africa won the series 1-0)

Ray Illingworth is not a man to deliver gushing praise, but even he was moved to describe Mike Atherton's match-saving heroics at the Wanderers as 'one of the great innings of all time'. When, on the fifth afternoon, Hansie Cronje finally accepted that the England captain's determination had defeated him, Atherton had been at the crease for 643 minutes, or ten-and-three-quarter hours. It was the fourth longest innings ever played for England and, surely, the performance of Atherton's life.

His decision at the start of the match to put South Africa in to bat had backfired. Led by Gary Kirsten's 110, South Africa rattled up 332 and England were dismissed for 200 in reply. McMillan's second-innings century gave South Africa a lead of 478 and England found themselves fighting for their lives before lunch on the fourth day. Atherton's wicket was the key. Through our headphones

in the commentary box we could hear the excitement of the South African fielders building up to a crescendo as, by the close, they captured four English wickets: Stewart, Ramprakash, Thorpe and Hick. The next morning Atherton, on 99, offered a sharp catch to short leg.

JONATHAN AGNEW: *'Atherton is on 99. And of course we're constantly being reminded that he is one of five batsmen who've been dismissed twice on 99, and if he's out for 99 he'll be the first player ever to be out for a third time on 99. Let's not think about that. The crowd here are building it all up rather nicely. Third man is still down there, two slips, a*

Recalled by Jonathan Agnew

Atherton was at the crease for nearly 11 hours – the fourth longest innings ever for England

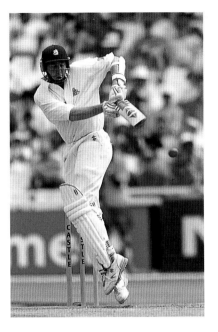

gully, there's a short leg — listen to the crowd as Donald runs in and bowls to Atherton, it's short … oh, he's dropped! Dropped at short leg! He fended it off straight into Gary Kirsten's tummy. It's one of those that either stick or doesn't, and on this occasion it didn't.

'He's still on 99, 210 for four, there goes Donald, bowls to Atherton and he hooks for four! As emphatic as you like. Atherton raises his arms. Ooh, he's giving Robin Smith a big hug. Well, that's all very nice. But it's been an excellent effort, and the South African fielders join in the applause for Mike Atherton, who's 103 not out. He's doing everything he can to try and save this match for England.'

Atherton did not give South Africa another chance. Smith, however, was caught at third man to keep a home victory very much the most likely outcome. But Jack Russell, who was dropped on five, hopped and scratched about, infuriating McMillan in particular, and he defended grimly for nearly four-and-three-quarter hours. In that time he scored just 29 runs while Atherton, whose concentration never wavered, finished unbeaten on 185.

JONATHAN AGNEW: *'Matches like this evoke so many memories. Watson and Bailey at Lord's, I suppose. Here's Eksteen, he*

bowls and that is the end of that over, the end of the 15, and Hansie Cronje shakes Jack Russell's hand — he has conceded. Mike Atherton raises his fist towards the England dressing room, he punches the air, handshakes all round.

'That is the end of a truly memorable Test Match. England have survived, they've lost just one wicket in the entire day and a joint Man of the Match has been awarded to Jack Russell and Mike Atherton. How about that!

'They're dashing for cover now, they've both got a stump, and what a Test Match it has been. There's bound to be great disappointment among the South Africans and who can blame them, they really did seem to have this match sewn up. But let's give credit to England. Many times over these past few years we've seen England fold under pressure and today what a magnificent effort by Mike Atherton.

'Another punch of the air as he walks off. He's being met there by his team-mates. Ray Illingworth too put an arm round him, a hug from Robin Smith. And here comes Jack Russell, who's still got his helmet on, he's still got his dark glasses on — he's batted in those throughout the day. And off he goes into the England dressing room.'

It was, without doubt, one of the greatest escape acts in Test history.

Atherton goes the distance, from left: A glance off his hip on the way to 185 not out; a hug from Robin Smith as he reaches 100 and Allan Donald despairs; and the triumphant conclusion, with arms round his partner in grim determination, Jack Russell

· BULAWAYO 1996 ·

Zimbabwe's great escape

'We flippin' murdered 'em!' ... Except somehow they managed to survive.
But Nick Knight's valiant assault on the last over so nearly won it for England
– and left a TMS commentary box full of quivering wrecks

ZIMBABWE v ENGLAND

BULAWAYO, 18-22 DECEMBER 1996

Zimbabwe 376	*A. Flower 112, A. D. R. Campbell 84*
England 406	*N. Hussain 113, J. P. Crawley 112,*
	N. V. Knight 56; P. A. Strang 5-123
Zimbabwe 234	*G. J. Whittall 56, A. C. Waller 50,*
	P. C. R. Tufnell 4-61
England 204-6	*N. V. Knight 96, A. J. Stewart 73*
Match drawn – scores level *(Series drawn 0-0)*	

It was beyond the dreams of the Zimbabwean Cricket Union that the inaugural Test Match against the 'Old Country' would finish with the scores level, match drawn. This quite remarkable cricket match in Bulawayo had a poor attendance and, due largely to two unfortunate incidents, has not received sufficient acclaim.

Out of desperation Zimbabwe resorted to the most negative tactics of bowling yards wide of the stumps on the final afternoon, which perhaps took the shine off their overall achievement. For England's part, the post-match claim by their coach David Lloyd that 'We murdered them' was neither charitable nor factual.

One man who kept his sense of occasion was Henry Blofeld, who gave the closing moments of this historic match what it deserved – and more.
He was so excited that he overran his half-hour spot by 45 minutes,

Recalled by Chris Cowdrey

A consoling pat for Nick Knight from Heath Streak, who bowled the dramatic final over oblivious to all requests to stand down from producer Peter Baxter, who also happened to be the in-coming commentator. There were no buses or pigeons, only jacaranda and Natal mahogany trees, yet Blowers was in vintage form.

What a match. The contest ebbed and flowed as England fought back superbly from a poor first day in the field, which witnessed a third Test century by Andy Flower and a sound batting display by Zimbabwe. Centurians Nasser Hussain and John Crawley led the England recovery, followed by some sharp out-cricket with the spinners Croft and Tufnell operating in tandem. They eventually prised out a stubborn Zimbabwean tail for a second time. So, 205 to win off a minimum of 75 overs.

Credit must be given to the England captain, Michael Atherton, for accepting the challenge, and although he was dismissed early himself, with Alec Stewart and Nick Knight still at the crease needing a further 87 off 15 overs, it looked plain sailing. England then lost Stewart, Hussain and Crawley in quick succession and clearly a run rate in excess of six an over with a new batsman at the crease was going to prove difficult with Zimbabwe bowling so deliberately wide.

Yet Knight batted superbly throughout the innings and at the start of the final over he and his partner Darren Gough required 13 to win. The TMS producer had made the executive decision not to disturb the wild beast during feeding time and Blowers was now in overdrive.

HENRY BLOFELD: *'And there's plenty of colourful greens and reds and golds in the crowd. And the crowd absolutely loving it – leaning over the fence standing on their feet. It's the third Test Match here at the Queens Club and they have never had one as exciting and tense as this. And it's going to be Heath Streak to bowl the last over. What a responsibility for him.*

'There is Heath Streak now coming in to bowl to Nick Knight. He is up to the wicket, he bowls, and Knight swings down the leg side and misses and that's a dot. So 13 needed from five balls and every Zimbabwean on the premises takes a huge sigh of relief. There are still five balls to go – five moments of excruciating and agonising suspense. What a game this is!

'Here is Heath Streak now – he's in, he bowls to Knight, who is down the wicket, who drives down to long on. They are going to get one, they are up for the second and they get it! It was a bad throw by the fielder there, Grant Flower. Very quick running but 11 now needed from four balls.'

CHRIS COWDREY: *'He panicked. He was worried about over-throws. No one is backing up – they're all 100 yards away.'*

The next ball left even Blofeld short of superlatives.

HENRY BLOFELD: *'Here is Streak again. He's in now, he bowls*

Nasser Hussain led the England reply to Zimbabwe's imposing first innings with his third Test century of 1996

to Knight, Knight plays this away. It's going for six runs! It's over the top, it's into the crowd, it's six! What a prodigious stroke. The Barmy Army can hardly believe it – they are jumping all over the place. Nick Knight picked it up and hit it far into the crowd at square leg and Paul Strang could only stand there and watch it go over his head. And now the equation is five runs from three balls.'

CHRIS COWDREY: 'Well, is that a Champagne Moment?'

HENRY BLOFELD: 'Oh my goodness me!'

CHRIS COWDREY: 'What a shot. That was about 80 yards.'

HENRY BLOFELD: 'And he hit it like a kicking horse. That almost brought the balloon down, it went so high. A wonderful blow. Now we are really going to take our time. Andy Flower is coming out from behind the stumps to have a word with Heath Streak. Alastair Campbell's coming over. Nick Knight is standing there looking entirely unconcerned. Darren Gough is merely thinking thank goodness I'm not in strike at the moment. David Lloyd is down below in front of us and looking as though he's got if not all the cares of the world on his shoulders, at least most of them. And what a moment for him.'

CHRIS COWDREY: 'I can see this being very wide, Heath Streak, miles down leg side. I'm sure Nick Knight is aware of that.'

HENRY BLOFELD: 'Well here he comes. It's Streak in to Knight and Knight can't reach that outside the off stump. Has umpire Robinson called a

There was nothing Heath Streak could do as Nick Knight struck the third ball of the last over for a sensational six (right). But the Zimbabwean seamer kept his cool

wide? Peter Baxter does in the box – but umpire Robinson certainly doesn't and I think actually it was a little bit exaggerated because Knight did move away to leg.

'Knight is standing there, Gough is giving him a little bit of advice. Knight has got 92, the score is 200 for five. Just five runs needed to win, two balls to be bowled. And here comes Heath Steak again, he's coming in off his short

run, he's bowling now. It's a full toss. Nick Knight scythes it down the ground, Grant Flower picks up, they're going to get two, he throws in… No! It can't be run out because the bowler Streak dropped the catch and took the bails off with his hand. So two more runs. Three are now needed off the last ball. Isn't it tremendous?'

CHRIS COWDREY: *'Sensational running from Darren Gough. He had to go, obviously, to give Knight the last ball.'*

HENRY BLOFELD: *'What's the betting someone's going to panic under the pressure of it. Goodness me, one ball to go, three runs to win, it's 202 for five, Nick Knight has got 94, Darren Gough has three, and absolutely everything is possible – not everything, obviously a Zimbabwe win isn't possible. What excitement!'*

CHRIS COWDREY: *'A tie isn't possible either, is it?'*

HENRY BLOFELD: *'No, this is a Test Match, not a one-day game. Anyway it all comes down to this, the last ball of the match. Five days have gone into it. Many many balls, much happening, and here comes the final ball. Three to win, and Streak is in, he bowls to Knight, Knight makes room and slogs this into the off side. It's fielded there at*

deep cover by Grant Flower, they're coming back and there's going to be a run-out! He is, he's run out! Gough has gone [in fact Knight was run out], the scores are level and the match is drawn. And Zimbabwe have got away with it.

'Knight is despondent, he's very sad, you can see his shoulders down as he walks off. Gough is striding out. The Zimbabweans are thrilled, they're congratulating everyone.

Alec Stewart helped Nick Knight to put England into a winning position. When it all went wrong, even the Barmy Army couldn't cheer up the disconsolate Knight

But what a game of cricket. Nick Knight steered England to the very brink of victory and couldn't quite get there. 204 for five, the scores level, but this was a Test Match and the game is drawn.

'So England by the narrowest of squeaks have failed to win this match. Now I think we should all go off to hospital to have our pulses checked.'

The most exciting climax to a Test Match had provided the perfect result – England on top, yet Zimbabwe able to celebrate an improbable draw in a match they did not deserve to lose.

Henry and I left the ground by taxi in total silence whilst we tried to absorb fully the extraordinary events of the final day of this inaugural Test Match in Bulawayo. After a while, Blowers rather sheepishly turned to me and said: 'Well old thing, was I all right? Did I upset the producer? Did I overstay my welcome?'

'No, no, no … well, yes, yes, yes, I suppose … but you were marvellous, Blowers.'

'Oh my dear old thing, thank you, so were you!'

Champagne Moments

LISTENERS AND COMMENTATORS RECALL THEIR FAVOURITE INCIDENTS FROM 40 YEARS OF TEST MATCH SPECIAL

My Champagne Moments:
1. John Arlott describing the run-up of Asif Masood of Pakistan as 'rather reminiscent of Groucho Marx chasing a waitress'.
2. Brian Johnston saying that if batsman and wicketkeeper missed the ball from a great Indian bowler, any runs should be recorded as 'Bedi byes'.
3. When a great Test player announced his retirement from Test cricket, Vic Marks turning to Jonathan Agnew to ask if he had announced *his* retirement from Test cricket.
— *Hugh Williams, West London*

Winter 1995-6: The description of Vic Marks and CMJ having to climb out of the Royal South African Golf Club when they had been inadvertently locked in.
— *Cynthia Floud, London NW3*

TEST MATCH SPECIAL
Quiz
• THE EIGHTIES •

7 Which England captain took his tally of Test victories over Australia to a record eleven?

Answer on page 120

Any time Fred Trueman is being grumpy about young cricketers not taking his advice.
— *John Phillips, Fishponds, Bristol*

E. W. SWANTON'S CHAMPAGNE MOMENT

A Boxing Day cracker

Christmas time 1938 saw the first-ever live broadcast of a Test Match back to England. It was at Johannesburg and I was the commentator, striving to keep listeners at home interested (after their Boxing Day lunch) in some pretty dull cricket.

Suddenly, ten minutes before close of play, Dudley Nourse hit a hard return catch into the capacious hands of Tom Goddard, the off-spinner. Alan Melville, the South African captain, sent in his tail-ender Norman Gordon, who promptly dragged his foot and was stumped by Les Ames.

Any fool of a broadcaster can make something of the prospect of a hat-trick. Billy Wade ultimately arrived at the crease and sure enough Tom bowled him with a quicker one. In those few minutes the game had swung round completely.

Hat-tricks have always been a rarity in Test cricket. England had only achieved five before, and only one other came between this one in 1938 and Dominic Cork's at Old Trafford two years ago. Goddard's is a Christmas memory I still savour.

I became addicted to TMS during the winter tour of Australia two or three years ago. I remember being glued to my radio to hear England actually win – four in the morning in pyjamas, and cans of Foster's strewn all over the floor as I leap around in a patriotic fever.

On a less lyrical note, Henry Blofeld revealing between spluttering chuckles that Robert Croft kept homing pigeons just about sums up the appeal of TMS for me.
— *Andy Taylor, Dublin*

My Champagne Moment: Gooch's 333. I was driving across the Pennines on a beautiful sunny day and I stopped somewhere on the tops, only me and lots of sheep, and listened to the cricket. The sheep were most surprised by this loony, waving and cheering.

And of course Johnners and Aggers laughing: it still makes me laugh.
— *Gwyneth Morgan, Bradford*

· THE LISTENERS' CHOICE ·

The Aggers and Johnners Legover Incident

The overwhelming favourite Champagne Moment, as far as TMS listeners are concerned, was Jonathan Agnew's description of how Ian Botham trod on his wicket – and Brian Johnston's reaction. We chose three of your letters to represent many, many more. Tony Cozier also selected it as his Champagne Moment...

ALAN AYCKBOURN:
My Champagne Moment would come anywhere during the 1981 Headingley Test Match against Australia – Botham's Test – either during his extraordinary innings or the Willis-inspired demolition which followed.

TONY COZIER'S CHAMPAGNE MOMENT

'Aggers, do stop it!'

There were countless moments during my many hours in the TEST MATCH SPECIAL commentary box that sparkled ... and most involved Brian Johnston, the heart and soul of the whole madcap operation. We were all, at some time or another, victims of his practical jokes – so I took special delight when his impish sense of humour completely got the better of him during the Oval Test in 1991.

Peter Baxter had then revived the system of summarising the day's play using two commentators to chat about it. The two this day were Johnners and Jonathan Agnew, in his first full season with TMS but even then an obvious graduate of the Johnston school of comedy. It was a dangerous combination.

When Aggers got to the incident where Ian Botham had got out by treading on his stumps after one especially ungainly hook, he said, not entirely innocently I'm sure,

---

Among thousands of gems, I must choose the moment when Jonathan Agnew and Brian Johnston were in fits of laughter after Botham was out and Agnew said that he 'didn't quite get his leg over'. Johnston was in such a state, and I remember being equally engulfed in laughter, and pulling up behind a police car at some roadworks in Peterborough. I could see the policeman looking at me in his rear-view mirror and he must have thought I was laughing at him. So much so, he got out and asked what I found so amusing – just as Johnston regained control of himself. I'm sure the policeman didn't believe me when I tried to explain what I'd just been listening to.

– *Paul Brookbanks, Peterborough*

The weather was glorious that summer and I had been confined to bed for several weeks with pneumonia. I felt very fed-up. Then I heard the 'legover' incident on TMS and for the first time in many weeks laughed ... until the tears streamed down my face.

– *Jane Wardman, Alwoodley, Leeds*

Aggers – Johnners – Leggers over.

– *John Ringrose, Sheffield*

---

that Botham 'just didn't quite get his leg over'.

It was all that was needed to set Johnners off. He gradually broke into uncontrollable giggling, his face turned redder and redder – and the summary, beamed live into millions of radios, became incomprehensible.

It must have gone on for a couple of minutes, which felt like a couple of hours.

I was seated next to them, in front of a dead microphone, amused by the hilarity but wondering what it must have sounded like to those driving down the M1 or in their living rooms in Barbados.

Johnners finally got his composure back, just, and completed the summary – only to berate me for not coming to his rescue. It did flash through my mind at the time ... but only for a split second.

Fortunately, I didn't butt in. The recording has now become part of TMS folklore. It shows Brian as I'll always remember him – a wonderful fun-loving man for whom a laugh and a giggle were never far away.

TEST MATCH SPECIAL
Quiz
· THE EIGHTIES ·

8 Who took seven England wickets in an innings with his left hand in plaster?

Answer on page 120

TMS Dream Teams

After forty years watching the greatest cricketers on Earth, our Test Match Special experts choose their World XI to take on Mars

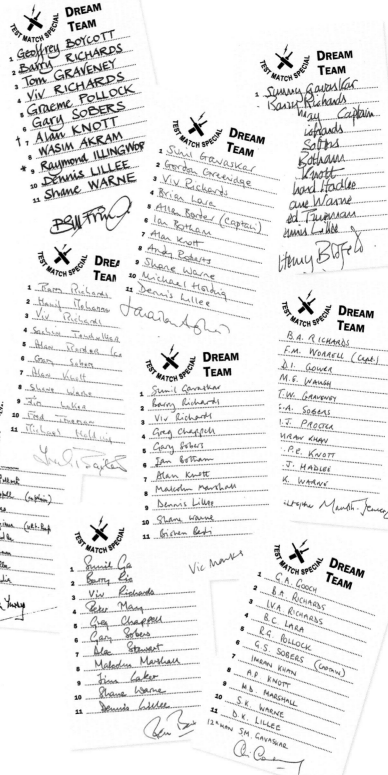

Jonathan Agnew

FROM 1957 TO 1997

I have only selected from players who I have actually seen 'live' in action — and I wasn't born when TMS started!

1 Sunil Gavaskar

The most complete opening batsman I have ever seen. Brave against fast bowling and quick, nimble and assertive against the spinners, which is by no means usual for an opener

2 Gordon Greenidge

Whenever his bad knee caused him to limp it was time for the bowlers to take cover: it was a signal that he had no intention of doing any running and would deal only in boundaries!

3 Vivian Richards

On his day — and he had a few — Viv was almost impossible to bowl at because of his extraordinary ability to flick deliveries from off stump through midwicket. The best batsman of his generation relished the fact that the bowlers knew it, too

4 Brian Lara

The most exquisite stroke-player with a flamboyant flourish of the bat. He is cricket's main attraction at the moment

5 Allan Border

There have been prettier players, but few with a determination to match the most capped cricketer in Test history. His ability to bowl slow left arm helped him into this Dream Team

6 Ian Botham

The most complete all-round cricketer of my generation and a player who had total self-belief. A match was never lost while Botham still had a part to play

7 Alan Knott

A wicketkeeper who had almost as many theories about cricket as Test victims (269). An infuriatingly unorthodox batsman, he scored precious runs for England in tight situations

8 Andy Roberts

A chillingly unemotional fast bowler whose expressionless glance at a batsman was more effective than any amount of sledging

9 Shane Warne

The man who has breathed new life into the mysterious art of wrist spin. Has there ever been a better delivery than the one which bowled Mike Gatting at Old Trafford in 1993?

10 Michael Holding

Fast bowling poetry in motion — as long as he was not sprinting in to bowl at you!

11 Dennis Lillee

What a bowling attack this is! Lillee is the master of modern-day fast bowling. He was the man, roaring in to bowl in 1972, who made me fall in love with cricket

Trevor Bailey

FROM 1957 TO 1997

The problem was whom to omit. This especially applied to the fast bowlers, because there have been so many of the highest class. I have therefore picked a balanced side by including both exciting strokemakers and grafters, a wicketkeeper who was brilliant standing up or back, as well as possessing the ability to score runs, an attack which would be formidable anywhere, and a decidedly volatile tail. Finally, in Gary Sobers I have the jewel in the crown, one of the finest batsmen in the history of the game, an outstanding left-arm seamer, probably the best wrist spinner in the world for about five years, and an orthodox finger spinner. He was also a super all-round fielder.

1 Barry Richards

The most technically correct batsman I ever bowled against, or have seen

2 Hanif Mohammad

The ideal sheet anchor with the required concentration

3 Viv Richards

Pure genius

4 Sachin Tendulkar

The finest 17-year-old I have ever seen, who probably has not yet reached his peak

5 Allan Border

In addition to his 11,174 runs in Test Matches and an average of 50, he was at his best in a crisis. A born fighter, as he showed when he came back from hospital with stitches in his head to complete his century. My choice as skipper

6 Gary Sobers

The finest all-rounder of all time

7 Alan Knott

Day in, day out, the most accomplished keeper I have seen

8 Shane Warne

The most complete leg-break and googly bowler since the war

9 Jim Laker *(right)*

The most successful off-spinner ever, with 193 wickets in only 46 Tests and almost 2,000 wickets in first-class cricket

10 Fred Trueman

The most colourful fast bowler since the war. The first to capture 300 wickets in Test cricket, he averaged five a game. He remained remarkably fit and finished with 2,304 wickets

11 Michael Holding

Not only the fastest bowler since Frank Tyson, but also the most beautiful to watch. On an Oval featherbed in 1976 he produced the finest piece of sustained fast bowling I have witnessed, taking 14 wickets for 149

Bailey on Laker:
'The most successful off-spinner ever, with 193 wickets in only 46 Tests'

Baxter on May:
'A commanding presence'

Peter Baxter
FROM 1957 TO 1997

I had more trouble selecting the bowling than the batting, though inevitably there were agonising decisions to be made in both areas...

1 **Sunil Gavaskar**
Neat, efficient, devastating accumulator of runs and a perfect foil for my No. 2

2 **Barry Richards**
How I wish we could have seen more of him at Test level. He might have been the best

3 **Viv Richards**
Imagine seeing him swagger in when you've got one of the first two out at last!

4 **Peter May** *(above)*
Captain. A commanding presence

5 **Greg Chappell**
I'd like to see a partnership between Nos. 4 and 5. I fancy there would be some fine straight driving

6 **Gary Sobers**
Surely the greatest all-rounder. I would perhaps have liked to see a left-hander before this

7 **Alec Stewart**
Wicketkeeper. This will be controversial, but I think he has earned it. I hope he can cope with Warne!

8 **Malcolm Marshall**
Quite a few candidates here, Lindwall, Trueman, Waqar Younis and many others, but I felt West Indies' fast bowling power had to be represented. Not a bad No. 8 batsman, either

9 **Jim Laker**
Surely the best off-spinner of the period

10 **Shane Warne**
With Sobers added, I've got a fair balance of top-class spin

11 **Dennis Lillee**
The best fast bowler I've seen

Henry Blofeld
FROM 1957 TO 1997

1 **Sunil Gavaskar**
A superb technician; brilliant against short-pitched fast bowling and the new ball. He had a fine array of strokes

2 **Barry Richards**
Surely no batsman could have made his art look simpler. If he had not been a victim of South Africa's ostracisation from Test cricket, he would have broken every record

3 **Peter May**
Captain. England's best post-war batsman. A classical stroke-maker who could dominate any attack whatever the situation

4 **Viv Richards**
A devastating batsman who destroyed the best of attacks and, like his South African namesake, able to score his runs at a prodigious rate in all conditions. Occasional off-spinner too

5 **Gary Sobers**
Quite simply the most staggering cricketer of all time. A brilliant left-handed batsman, left arm over the wicket fast bowler, orthodox left-arm spinner, unorthodox left-arm spinner and brilliant fielder. Enough said

6 **Ian Botham**
Another instinctive and dynamic all-rounder with the ability to turn a match with bat or ball in a handful of overs

7 **Alan Knott**
A genius in wicketkeeping gloves, whether standing up or back. A keeper who inspired his fielders and was at his best standing up to a spinner, particularly Derek Underwood on a drying pitch. Scored five Test centuries

8 **Richard Hadlee**
Arguably the best fast-medium seam bowler ever, whose variation and control was good enough to bring him 431 Test wickets. A good enough batsman, too, to rank as a genuine all-rounder

9 **Shane Warne**
Probably the greatest leg-spinner of all. He has immense variety and astonishing control and is a fierce competitor

10 **Dennis Lillee**
The best fast bowler I have seen. He had a wonderful rhythmic action, a peach of an out-swinger and later a devastating leg-cutter as well as an inherent hatred of batsmen

11 **Fred Trueman**
The first bowler to take 300 Test wickets. A glorious action, a remarkable late out-swinger and a great striking rate: 307 wickets in only 67 Tests. Also a fine close-to-the-wicket fielder

TEST MATCH SPECIAL DREAM TEAM
Chris Cowdrey
FROM 1957 TO 1997

1 **Gooch** *(right)*
I am full of admiration for the way he has retained his zest for the game – and his hair for that matter. Just pipped Greenidge and Gavaskar

2 **Richards B**
The most effortless timer of the ball. Batting with Gooch will teach him to be more greedy for runs

3 **Richards V**
Awaiting his arrival into the arena was always a moment of great suspense. The entrance of the most savage, destructive batsman of them all was pure theatre

4 **Lara**
I wanted a left-hander at No. 3 but Viv wouldn't budge

5 **Pollock**
Seldom have I seen anyone with such a wide bat. What a shame that politics robbed us of him and Richards at their best

6 **Sobers**
The best cricketer of all time. He may open the bowling, bowl spin, catch everything, bat anywhere as well as captain the side

7 **Imran Khan**
The complete all-rounder – his batting edges out Hadlee, but I cringe at the thought of omitting Ian Botham and particularly Mike Procter

8 **Knott**
The best wicketkeeper-batsman. Watch him standing up to Shane Warne and Garfield Sobers – remember him to Underwood on a wet one

9 **Marshall**
Holding, Roberts, Garner, Daniel, Croft, Ambrose, Walsh, Hall, Griffith, Clarke, Benjamin … not for me

10 **Warne**
His Test record to date says it all

11 **Lillee**
The smooth approach, the perfect action, the aggressive appealing – which end do you want, DK?

Twelfth man: Gavaskar. 10,122 Test runs in 125 Tests at an average of 51.12. Sorry, Sunil, you're carrying the drinks!

TEST MATCH SPECIAL DREAM TEAM
Tony Cozier
FROM 1957 TO 1997

1 **Sunil Gavaskar**
Eulogised in Caribbean Calypso as 'The Real Master', the West Indies saw more of him than any other batsman as he compiled 13 of his 34 Test hundreds against us!

2 **Gordon Greenidge**
Ted Dexter described him as the best right-handed batsman of his time, high praise indeed. He usually established the foundation of the West Indies innings, first with Roy Fredericks, then in his long association with Desmond Haynes

3 **Viv Richards**
There was no one with a more awesome presence on a cricket field. Even his stride to the wicket was menacing and once there, he had the sole intention of destroying the opposition

4 **Javed Miandad**
Like Allan Border, Javed loved a crisis. His wristy improvisation and cheeky manner drove opponents to despair

5 **Greg Chappell**
Most West Indian bowlers who played against them rate Ian as the Chappell they would most want to get out, but I always felt better when Greg was gone. Or worse, because he made his runs so elegantly. And at an average of 53.86.

6 **Gary Sobers**
A phenomenon, the likes of whom I don't expect to see again. No one did more on a cricket field, nor did it more gracefully. It is a physical marvel that, for all he achieved, he played 85 of his 93 Tests over 17 years without missing a match

7 **Allan Knott**
If Knotty missed a chance in his 22 Tests against the West Indies, I didn't notice it

8 **Imran Khan** *(right)*
Imran reserved his best for the West Indies. His duels with Greenidge, Richards and Lloyd with the ball, and with Roberts, Marshall and Ambrose with the bat, are unforgettable

9 **Malcolm Marshall**
Ditto for Lillee except Marshall was shorter and seemed to skid through faster, which made his bouncer more dangerous. Only Ian Botham of his era swerved the ball both ways so effectively

10 **Dennis Lillee**
Swing, pace, cut, intelligence, aggression, Lillee had it all

11 **Lance Gibbs**
It was stimulating to watch Gibbs wheeling away at an over a minute, wrapping his long fingers round the ball to impart maximum spin, varying pace and flight and ever aggressive and combative, convinced every ball was worth a wicket

Cozier on Imran:
'His duels with Greenidge, Richards and Lloyd with the ball, and with Roberts, Marshall and Ambrose with the bat, are unforgettable'

Fowler on Sobers: 'A sublime and complete cricketer in every way'

Gerald De Kock
FROM 1957 TO 1997

1 **Barry Richards**
The most complete opener of the modern era, capable of destroying any new-ball attack with breathtaking strokeplay

2 **Sunil Gavaskar**
A wonderful technique against fast bowling; an accumulator supreme ... with a huge heart

3 **Vivian Richards**
An awesome hitter with great technique and fierce pride

4 **Graeme Pollock**
Tall left-hander with superb timing and an ability to score big hundreds

5 **Ian Botham**
An all-rounder who could turn a match in a couple of overs with bat or ball: he made things happen

6 **Sir Garfield Sobers** *(below)*
The most complete all-rounder; left-handed batsman with power and grace – and could bowl pace or spin

7 **Ray Jennings**
A tall slim wicketkeeper; wonderful hands and incredible agility; very smooth mover

8 **Shane Warne**
A leg-spinner with great control and huge variety; bowls wicket-taking deliveries regularly; aggresive low-order hitter

9 **Sir Richard Hadlee**
Accuracy, swing and seam at high pace; superb use of the old ball; skillful left-handed batsman

10 **Malcolm Marshall**
Extreme pace and aggression combined with the mastery of movement; also fine change of pace

11 **Dennis Lillee**
Raw aggression combined with true pace; classic action produces steep bounce and high strike rate

Graeme Fowler
FROM 1957 TO 1997

1 **Sunil Gavaskar**
Great poise and control

2 **Barry Richards**
The most gifted player I have ever seen

3 **Viv Richards**
The most destructive batsman – and his fielding wasn't bad

4 **Javed Miandad**
Unorthodox but consistent genius

5 **Clive Lloyd**
Pure power and the greatest manager ever

6 **Ian Botham**
The best Test Match-winner the game has known

7 **Gary Sobers**
Sublime and complete cricketer in every aspect

8 **Shane Warne**
Has taken the art of spin bowling to a new level

9 **Alan Knott**
Never missed anything

10 **Joel Garner**
Incredibly awkward to bat against and faster than people realised

11 **Dennis Lillee**
A cricketer's cricketer and a fast bowler's bowler

*Twelfth man: Roger Harper.
The best all-round fielder I have seen*

Alan Knott stumps Lawrence Rowe: 'He never missed anything'

TEST MATCH SPECIAL DREAM TEAM
Bill Frindall
FROM 1957 TO 1997

Dream Teams usually feature Attila The Hun as a fast bowler and Adolf Hitler as the demon all-rounder. Under the severe limitations imposed by our producer/editor, I have reluctantly restricted my choices to players whose exploits I have chronicled during my 31 summers as the TMS scorer. Apart from my first selection, I have chosen the players who have given me most pleasure.

1 **Geoffrey Boycott**
A statistician's dream – broke most of the records but scored so slowly that I had ample time to look them up

2 **Barry Richards**
Versatile batting genius who would surely have rewritten the record books had he been permitted a full Test career

3 **Tom Graveney**
The most elegant batting artist of my time, he even hooked fast bowling off the front foot

4 **Viv Richards**
Deservedly dubbed the Master Blaster

5 **Graeme Pollock**
A more powerful, robust, left-handed version of Graveney

6 **Sir Garfield Sobers**
Dominated my first TMS series in 1966, scoring 722 runs, taking 20 wickets, holding 10 catches and winning all five tosses

7 **Alan Knott**
A genuine all-rounder: the best wicketkeeper since Godfrey Evans and an immensely entertaining improviser with the bat

8 **Wasim Akram**
Another left-handed all-rounder, capable of scoring 257 in a Test Match and a pace bowler with lethal late swing who should soon become the top wicket-taker in Test history

9 **Raymond Illingworth**
Captain. Yet another all-rounder. Militantly professional and always right, he combined meanly accurate off-spin with courageous middle-order batting and aggressive gully fielding

10 **Dennis Lillee**
He was a formidable sight, hair flowing like Keith Miller, as he bounded towards the unfortunate batsman

11 **Shane Warne**
The most gifted spinner of a ball on any surface I have seen. If his shoulder and fingers can stand the strain, he should succeed Wasim Akram as the leading Test wicket-taker

Twelfth man: Jonty Rhodes. A superb fielder

Commentator: John Arlott. Unique blend of full-bodied voice, ex-policeman's powers of observation, poet's gift of description and a great empathy with cricketers and the game itself

Frindall on Lillee:
'A formidable sight, hair flowing like Keith Miller, as he bounded towards the unfortunate batsman'

A trio of fine bowlers selected for the Bearded Wonder XI: Dennis Lillee, Wasim Akram celebrating his 300th Test wicket, Ray Illingworth

Marks on Bedi:

'Would not spend too long bowling over the wicket into the rough outside leg stump'

TEST MATCH SPECIAL DREAM TEAM
Robert Hudson
FROM 1957 TO 1997

My object was to select a balanced team, with all seven major Test-playing countries represented, so is not necessarily the strongest available side in the 40-year period — e.g. no Compton, Cowdrey or Trueman!

1 **B. A. Richards**
2 **G. Greenidge**
3 **P. B. H. May**
4 **Viv Richards**
5 **M. Azharuddin**
6 **G. Sobers**
7 **I. T. Botham**
8 **Mushtaq Mohammad**
9 **R. Benaud**
10 **Sir R. Hadlee**
11 **T. G. Evans**

TEST MATCH SPECIAL DREAM TEAM
David Lloyd
FROM 1957 TO 1997

Team selected from players I have seen. Don't need a captain — field where you want, bowl when you want! (Sorry!!!! Akram, Marshall, Miandad, etc, etc.)

1 **Gavaskar**
2 **Gooch**
3 **Richards I. V. A.**
4 **Lara**
5 **Tendulkar** *(below)*
6 **Sobers**
7 **Botham**
8 **Knott**
9 **Warne**
10 **Holding**
11 **Lillee**

TEST MATCH SPECIAL DREAM TEAM
Vic Marks
FROM 1957 TO 1997

1 **Sunil Gavaskar**
On the field a little master; off it a little mischievous. Has opened the bowling for his country, which would not be necessary in this side

2 **Barry Richards**
Offers technical perfection and grace. It was a misfortune — not a tragedy — for cricket lovers and for Richards himself that he did not play more Test cricket

3 **Viv Richards**
The best batsman I played with or against. He could will himself to 100s when it really mattered

4 **Greg Chappell**
Captain. Arguably the second best batsman in Australia's history and the second best captain in his family

5 **Gary Sobers**
Effortless left-handed genius who could do everything

6 **Ian Botham**
Away swing bowler; forceful right-handed bat; useful slip fieldsman; keen competitor

7 **Alan Knott**
Would conduct the team's early morning stretches, catch the nicks and sweep opposition spinners to distraction

8 **Malcolm Marshall**
Capable of extreme speed and guile. Broken bones in his body did not deter him from wreaking havoc (Headingley 1984)

9 **Dennis Lillee**
Capable of extreme speed and guile. A busted back did not deter him

10 **Shane Warne**
The most prodigious spinner of a cricket ball that I have ever witnessed and one of the most accurate. Scowls when hit for four

11 **Bishan Bedi** *(right)*
Would not spend too long bowling over the wicket into the rough outside leg stump. Mesmerising left-arm spinner. Often applauded batsmen when hit for four

TEST MATCH SPECIAL DREAM TEAM
Christopher Martin-Jenkins
FROM 1957 TO 1997

1 **Barry Richards**
When there was a real challenge this wonderfully felicitous batsman would rise to it with a viruoso's ease and grace

2 **Frank Worrell**
My captain and a batsman of class and grace who would maintain the game's dignity at all times, on and off the field, not least in tense contests against Mars

3 **David Gower**
Grace, charm and entertainment value have been my criteria for deciding between all the great players available. David had all three

4 **Mark Waugh**
In the toughest circumstances he looks cool and effortless; like my other batsmen he makes batting look beautiful

5 **Tom Graveney**
Pure prejudice here. Tom was my boyhood hero and the epitome of elegance. He also scored 122 centuries

6 **Gary Sobers**
The greatest of all the all-rounders and the team's automatic pivot

7 **Mike Procter**
I hate to leave out Ian Botham, but when the force was with Procter with the ball he was even more irresistible – and he was a most glorious batsman too

8 **Imran Khan**
Skill, intelligence, speed and power. He takes the new ball as Procter's partner, again just ahead of Botham, whose equal he also was with the bat

9 **Alan Knott**
At least as good as any 'keeper there has been and ideal in the highly unlikely event of a batting crisis

10 **Richard Hadlee**
Even ahead of Dennis Lillee, Hadlee in his years of maturity was the supreme bowling technician of the last 40 years

11 **Shane Warne**
I hate to omit my favourite spin bowler, Bishan Bedi, but no one has spun the ball more viciously with such amazing accuracy as 'Shine' and he deserves the accolade for resurrecting the art of wrist spin, thus restoring much of the variety and fascination of Test cricket

TEST MATCH SPECIAL DREAM TEAM
Don Mosey
FROM 1957 TO 1997

1 **Geoffrey Boycott**
Regrettable, but he has to be included for his technique if not his personality

2 **Sunil Gavaskar**
His run-scoring record speaks for itself – and, as a personality, he could compensate for his partner

3 **Vivian Richards** (below)
The destroyer of bowling of all kinds

4 **Graeme Pollock**
The greatest left-hand bat of the post-war years

5 **Greg Chappell**
Captain. Outstanding batsman and close catcher

6 **Gary Sobers**
The greatest all-rounder of the modern era. Apart from his huge batting talents, he could contribute three kinds of bowling and outstanding close catching

7 **Farokh Engineer**
Wicketkeeper. Could do a good job batting anywhere in the order

8 **Richard Hadlee**
Ranks (almost) as an all-rounder at international level – and what a third seamer to back up the next two bowlers!

9 **Fred Trueman**
England's greatest fast-bowling product; another close catcher; and he made three first-class centuries

10 **Dennis Lillee**
Australia's greatest fast bowler since Ray Lindwall

11 **Abdul Qadir**
Leg spinner of infinite variety

Mosey on Richards: 'The destroyer of bowling of all kinds'

Fred Trueman:

'For me to try to pick a team would be completely and utterly unfair. I could pick 150 people that have given us great pleasure throughout those forty years, so I would decline the offer to be that selector.'

TEST MATCH SPECIAL DREAM TEAM
Neville Oliver
FROM 1957 TO 1997

I didn't quite realise how difficult this task was until I started looking at the players available...

Openers: This pairing was a very difficult decision to make, but believing the chemistry of an opening partnership is as or more important than the individuals, this pair is the stand-out.

1 **Desmond Haynes**

2 **Gordon Greenidge**

3 **Sunil Gavaskar**

   The prince of openers could bat at No. 3 for me

Middle order: Apologies to the fifty players who could justify their existence here very easily. To overlook the likes of Miandad, Border, Richards and my own favourite, impossible to get out, Ken Barrington, seems both unfair and almost totally illogical.

4 **Graeme Pollock**

   Robbed of a substantial part of his Test career but I suspect all the world's great recent players would have him in their side

5 **Greg Chappell** *(below)*

   As elegant and as technically sound as a batsman could be

6 **Gary Sobers**

   Quite simply the best player I have been privileged to see

7 **Rodney Marsh**

   'Old Iron Gloves' was a useful batsman and an absolutely outstanding keeper

Fast bowlers: Again apologies to many. These three fast bowlers are an entirely subjective judgement but a pretty lethal attack. Fred Trueman won't speak to me again and Holding, Roberts, Garner, Kapil Dev, Jeff Thomson, etc, etc, could feel aggrieved.

8 **Richard Hadlee**

9 **Dennis Lillee**

10 **Malcolm Marshall**

11 **Shane Warne**

   The only current player. A match-winner who reminded the cricketing world that there was another dimension to the game after four fast bowlers sending down seventy overs per day

---

TEST MATCH SPECIAL DREAM TEAM
Mike Selvey
FROM 1957 TO 1997

Taken from my time as a TMS summariser, which began in Bombay, December 1994. This is the team I would pay good money to go and watch. I'm assuming the game is being played at Lord's. If played on the subcontinent, then substitute Waqar for Hadlee, Imran for Botham, and Abdul Qadir for Marshall. No place alas for Tendulkar (he ought to be there instead of Azhar but I could spend all day watching that whippy thing he plays through square leg), Gooch, Gower, Border, Boon, Crowe, Miandad or Richardson or for Ambrose, Walsh, Kapil Dev or Mushtaq Ahmed.

1 **Sunil Gavaskar**

2 **Gordon Greenidge**

3 **Viv Richards**

4 **Brian Lara**

5 **Mohammed Azharuddin**

6 **Ian Botham** *(right)*

7 **Ian Healy**

8 **Wasim Akram**

9 **Richard Hadlee**

10 **Malcolm Marshall**

11 **Shane Warne**

LARA Doesn't give a XXXX about WARNE

Well, they agree with at least one of your selections, Mike

TEST MATCH SPECIAL DREAM TEAM
E. W. Swanton
FROM 1957 TO 1997

I have picked the following not as the best, but for the qualities of attraction and personality. I would greatly enjoy watching this side whether batting or in the field. All have played Test cricket over the period 1957-97.

1 **S. M. Gavaskar**
2 **Sir Colin Cowdrey**
3 **B. C. Lara**
4 **Sir Garfield Sobers**
5 **E. R. Dexter**
6 **Sir F. M. Worrell (capt)**
7 **T. G. Evans**
8 **R. R. Lindwall**
9 **S. K. Warne**
10 **J. C. Laker**
11 **W. W. Hall**

Twelfth man: R. N. Harvey
Reserves: D. I. Gower, L. R. Gibbs, A. K. Davidson

Trevor Bailey watches Ray Lindwall but decides not to select him

TEST MATCH SPECIAL DREAM TEAM
Bryan Waddle
FROM 1957 TO 1997

I have selected my Dream Team only from players I have seen play. My openers have been chosen as a partnership, in the belief that Greenidge and Haynes were the most effective opening pair, slightly ahead of most long-standing pairings. Sadly that of course prevents me selecting such players as Gavaskar and Hanif Mohammad. I have chosen 12 and depending on the pitch would probably have to make Fred twelfth man.

1 **Gordon Greenidge** *(below)*
2 **Desmond Haynes**
3 **Ian Chappell**
4 **Viv Richards**
5 **Graeme Pollock**
6 **Garfield Sobers**
7 **Ian Botham**
8 **Alan Knott**
9 **Richard Hadlee**
10 **Dennis Lillee**
11 **Shane Warne**
12 **Fred Trueman**

AND THE ULTIMATE TEST MATCH SPECIAL DREAM TEAM

1 **Sunil Gavaskar**
   (14 votes out of 18)
2 **Barry Richards**
   (10 votes)
3 **Vivian Richards**
   (15 votes)
4 **Greg Chappell**
   (7 votes)
5 **Graeme Pollock**
   (7 votes)
6 **Gary Sobers**
   (17 votes)
7 **Ian Botham**
   (9 votes)
8 **Alan Knott**
   (11 votes)
9 **Richard Hadlee**
   (9 votes)
10 **Dennis Lillee**
   (14 votes)
11 **Shane Warne**
   (16 votes)

Twelfth man:
Gordon Greenidge
(7 votes)

Not a bad line-up.
The TMS commentary team
hereby challenges them
to a charity match!

Champagne Moments

LISTENERS AND COMMENTATORS RECALL THEIR FAVOURITE INCIDENTS FROM 40 YEARS OF TEST MATCH SPECIAL

IAN CARMICHAEL:

1. 1953 England v Australia at Lord's. At 12.42pm on the final day, Trevor Bailey joined Willie Watson with England on 73 for four, needing 270 to avoid defeat. Four-and-a-half hours later the partnership was broken, with only 40 minutes to stumps. When it began Lord's was nearly empty. By the time Bailey was out for 71, people had poured in. A nail-biting Champagne afternoon.

2. 1956 Australia v Surrey at The Oval. Jim Laker, in a marathon spell of four hours, took 10 for 88 after having been up all the previous night at the birth of a

TEST MATCH SPECIAL
Quiz
• THE NINETIES •

9 Who was out 'handled the ball' in the 1994 Ashes series?

Answer on page 120

PETER BAXTER'S CHAMPAGNE MOMENT

'We've got a freaker'

A hot afternoon at Lord's, 1975, England versus Australia. In the commentary box, John Arlott has returned from a very good lunch with his publisher and is feeling on top form. He has added incentive to play a few shots, as the Managing Director of BBC Radio is visiting us in the box.

Suddenly there is a commotion from the Tavern area. Trevor Bailey spots him first. 'Ah! A freaker!' A well-fleshed and utterly naked young man is running for the middle of Lord's. (The term 'streaker' is still relatively new to some of us.)

Arlott takes up the theme. 'We've got a freaker. Not very shapely – and it's masculine. And I would think it's seen the last of its cricket for the day. The police are mustered; so are the cameramen and Greg Chappell. He's being embraced by a blond policeman and this may be his last public appearance, but what a splendid one.

'He's now being marched down in the final exhibition past at least eight thousand people in the Mound Stand, some of whom, perhaps, have never seen anything quite like this before.'

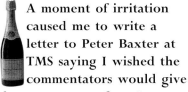

A moment of irritation caused me to write a letter to Peter Baxter at TMS saying I wished the commentators would give the score more often. I was amused to receive a hand-written letter from the producer himself saying that he had the same problem!
– *G. H. Taylor, Warfield, Berks*

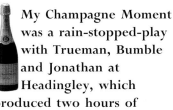

My Champagne Moment was a rain-stopped-play with Trueman, Bumble and Jonathan at Headingley, which produced two hours of magnificent impromptu chat in which Trueman revealed a knowledge of cricketers past and present which was staggering. Especially do I remember his Wally Hammond anecdotes. I wanted the rain to go on.
– *Michael D. Flynn, Burton on Trent*

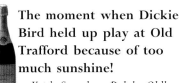

The moment when Dickie Bird held up play at Old Trafford because of too much sunshine!
– *Keith Saunders, Delph, Oldham*

BRYAN WADDLE'S CHAMPAGNE MOMENT

Snap, crackle and pop

TEST MATCH SPECIAL used to reach New Zealand via a crackle of short wave. Through the fluctuating radio reception, a crowd's ovation was more often than not a wake-up call to remind you that you had just missed an important feature of the Test!

Few New Zealanders will forget Jeremy Coney's boundary off Ian Botham that won New Zealand's first ever Test in England in 1983.

Even before that, Richard Collinge's dismissal of Geoffrey Boycott at Wellington's Basin Reserve which set NZ on the road to the first win over England after 48 Tests and 48 years of trying remains a lasting memory.

But success isn't the only thing that generates pride and passion for one's sport and country. In the mind's eye, defeat often endures longer than victory.

So I'll choose a very recent memory that falls in between – Nathan Astle and Danny Morrison defiantly denying England victory at Eden Park in 1997.

On Monday 4 December 1995, one of my favourite innings was played by the England captain Mike Atherton. With six wickets left on the last day, England were 312 runs behind on an ever-shifting wicket. Nobody would ever have betted on them saving the game. Atherton batted for nearly 11 hours and ended up with 185 not out, valiantly supported by wicketkeeper Jack Russell. It was one long, glorious Champagne Moment!

— *Nick Reed (aged 12), Southport*

Any occasion when Brian Johnston gently brought Fred Trueman back to reality was a Champagne Moment. Dear Fred's memory is so rose-tinted, and as his criticisms of players' behaviour became ever more sanctimonious, Brian would interject: 'Of course you never ever showed your feelings at such moments, did you Fred?' Collapse of stout party.

Brian's gift for defusing heated feelings without ever appearing to put the talker's back up was one of his greatest gifts. In the same way he would deflect the boring or the pompous. One was left always with a smile. Never did he expose anyone to ridicule. What a unique talent he had!

— *Mrs Anne Rowntree, Streatham, London*

DON MOSEY'S CHAMPAGNE MOMENT

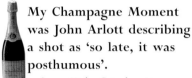

A visitor's voice of history

Eighteen summers of broadcasting in TEST MATCH SPECIAL brought the happiest moments of my working life and it would be quite impossible to single out one experience which was better than all the others. So, being a bit of a history buff, I have chosen a moment which gave me a personal place in history.

It was the morning of 15 February 1978 and I went to the Basin Reserve in Wellington to see New Zealand complete the formalities of a first-ever Test win over England. I said to my friend Alan Richards, cricket correspondent of Radio New Zealand: 'This is your day. I am happy to be here to see it happen but I want no part in the radio commentary this morning. You and Iain (Gallaway) and Trevor (Rigby) take over.'

The New Zealanders, who are the most generous hosts in the world, would have none of this and insisted on sticking to the scheduled rota. And inevitably this meant that when Richard Hadlee took the last wicket, it was the Pom's voice describing it for NZ listeners. It's there, for ever more, in the archives of Radio New Zealand. I can never escape the feeling of regret that it was not a Kiwi voice describing that moment.

Nor was my conscience eased when, a few years later, I saw a North of England XV beat Graham Mourie's All Blacks at Otley. And whose voice was it describing that moment…?

A heated debate from some years ago between Tony Lewis and Tony Cozier concerning the West Indies bowlers' slow over rates.

The rate should be quickened, said Tony Lewis.

Okay, said Tony Cozier, we'll quicken the rate … and bowl England out sooner!

— *R. Wild, Stockport, Cheshire*

My Champagne Moment was John Arlott describing a shot as 'so late, it was posthumous'.

— *Barry Kirk, Grimsby, Lincs*

A bit of licence here, if I may: Botham's 149 not out at Leeds v Australia in 1981. New to Evesham then, with my husband travelling, I was short of company and, turning the radio dial, discovered TEST MATCH SPECIAL.

I was gripped by the sheer improbability of the situation, even taking a portable radio to the woods to walk my Irish setter … and have been hooked on cricket ever since.

So a Champagne Day, really, because that innings sparked an interest that has brought me much pleasure and a whole host of friends – including the TMS team.

Many happy returns!

— *Anne Conolly, Evesham, Worcs*

FROM OPPOSITE PAGE daughter. The first of his Champagne Moments that season.

3. 1957 England v West Indies at Edgbaston. England entered their second innings 288 runs behind. At 113 for three, Cowdrey joined May in a match-saving partnership of 411. Champagne indeed.

4. 1963 England v West Indies at Lord's. The final afternoon was as exciting as any I have seen, as Cowdrey went to bat with his arm in plaster and Allen played out Hall's final ball for the draw. Earlier, on his way to 70, Brian Close took ball after ball from Hall and Griffith on his body to avoid committing himself to a stroke. A Champagne Moment – though not, I feel sure, for D. B. Close.

TEST MATCH SPECIAL *Quiz* • THE NINETIES •

10 Which England batsman has twice been out for 99?

Answer on page 120

Looking forward to another century

WILL WE STILL BE TUNING IN TO HEAR NEW VOICES
DESCRIBING NEW FEATS IN 40 YEARS' TIME?
THE BBC'S CRICKET CORRESPONDENT POLISHES UP HIS CRYSTAL BALL

BY Jonathan Agnew

*i*f there is one thing the last 40 years of TEST MATCH SPECIAL has proved, it is that our audience is remarkably loyal and resilient. This has particularly been the case in the past decade, when the programme's future has been under threat.

In the early 1990s there were no fewer than four frequency changes in as many years. Listeners were not only expected to change the wavelength they were used to, but even the wave band while TMS moved from Radio 3 Medium Wave to Radio 3 FM and then from Radio 5 on the medium wave to Radio 4 Long Wave. In fact, considering all of that, it is astonishing that we have any listeners left!

Yet we can still look out of our commentary box windows and see row upon row of spectators basking in the sunshine with their headphones firmly strapped on, confirming that cricket enthusiasts will overcome any hurdle in order to follow the game they love.

I really believe that our current home, on Radio 4 Long Wave, has benefited TEST MATCH SPECIAL considerably – though I fully accept that the programme is not what it was. There are frequent interruptions for shipping forecasts, and there are some programmes on Radio 4 which are regarded as sacrosant and therefore must be transmitted on both FM and long wave. The *Today* programme and *The Archers*, for example, often interfere with our commentary from England's winter tours. However, for reasons I will explain shortly, TEST MATCH SPECIAL will return to the way it was and it will survive. In fact, I believe that it will do more than that; it will flourish thanks to our short stop-over on Radio 4.

TEST MATCH SPECIAL is one of the most effective means of attracting people to cricket. The first time I became aware of the game was as a youngster following my father about on his farm as the voices of John Arlott, Johnners and Co crackled out from his little portable radio. Throughout the cricketing world – and particularly in the Caribbean and Asia – the sight of clusters of people gathered round a radio which is loudly blaring out cricket commentary is a familiar one. I am truly staggered by the number of blind listeners, many of whom, tragically, have never seen a cricket match in their lives, who adore TEST MATCH SPECIAL.

The combination of cricket and chat makes the programme irresistible to a great many people and now, I am delighted to say, to a rapidly increasing female audience.

This is largely because of our move to Radio 4. We go on the air during the hugely successful *Woman's Hour* and many listeners stay with us. My postbag during the early months of our first summer on Radio 4 was inundated with letters from ladies who were outraged by our intrusion. By July, the tone had changed very noticeably to: 'I know we cannot get rid of you and, surprisingly, I find myself rather enjoying your company. Perhaps you can tell me what on earth a silly mid-off is?'

Now, two years on, half the people who write to me are women. That is a terrific response and comes at a time when, for the first time, a great deal of money from England's main sponsor, Vodafone, is being channelled into women's cricket, which I hope will have good reason to thank Radio 4 and TEST MATCH SPECIAL in the future as more and more women take up the sport. And this is why I am

'My postbag in the early months on Radio 4 was largely from ladies outraged by our intrusion.
By July, the tone had changed to: "I know we cannot get rid of you and, surprisingly, I find myself rather enjoying your company. Can you tell me what on earth a silly mid-off is?"'

so optimistic about the future of TEST MATCH SPECIAL; we have a bigger audience than ever and soon we will have a new home of our very own which will be as secure as Fort Knox (or nearly, at least!).

Digital Audio Broadcasting (DAB) is the future of broadcasting. Just as compact discs have revolutionised the way we enjoy listening to music at home, so DAB offers the same crystal-clear sound – but on radio. The reception on car receivers will not be affected by driving under bridges, through tunnels or even in underground car parks, and literally hundreds of radio stations will transmit in this manner. Rather than tuning in to Radio 2, for instance, we will select 'Popular Music' on our receivers and be offered a host of channels, including Radio 2. One of these, under 'Radio Sport' and on its own dedicated channel throughout both summer and winter, will be TEST MATCH SPECIAL.

It will not happen overnight, but it will happen some time (ten years from now seems to be a reasonable estimate). DAB 'Walkmen', which can be carried about and used with earphones, will be produced. Car DAB receivers are already being manufactured.

It is the light at the end of the tunnel and should ensure that in the year 2037, TEST MATCH SPECIAL will be celebrating its eightieth birthday. I only hope that I am still around to enjoy it!

Don't be surprised if the TMS team of 2037 is reporting on action like this: England wicketkeeper Jane Smit goes for the catch as Belinda Clark of Australia throws the bat against England during the 1993 World Cup

ALLSPORT:

Jacket: CMJ, Botham, Warne; 6 Cowdrey; 10 Arlott; 11 Blowers fans, CMJ; 12 Gough; 14-15 Barmy Army, Dexter, Botham; 18 Compton, Bradman; 21 Laker; 24 Illingworth; 28 CMJ; 29 Billboard; 32 Chandrasekhar; 33 Greig; 34 Marks; 35 Garner, Richards; 36-7 Amiss, Gatting sequence; 38 Botham, Gooch, Gower; 40-1 Cowdrey, Barmy Army, sunglasses; 42 Court scenes; 43 Wasim, Waqar; 44 Players, third umpire; 45 Lara, Cork, Warne; 49 Commentary box;

Right: Decca Recording Studios, 1971. Johnners conducts the England cricket team as they record their version of that unforgettable song 'The Ashes' following their series win in Australia. The composer of the lyrics was one B. A. Johnston

64 Swanton; 76 Botham, Brearley, Dilley, Willis; 77 Dilley; 78 Botham; 79 Botham; 82 Ranatunga, De Mel; 83 Madugalle, De Silva; 84 Thomson; 85 Border, Miller; 86 Greenidge, Botham; 87 Greenidge, Gomes; 88 Gower, Robinson; 89 Gavaskar; 90 Lamb; 91 Gooch, Gooch; 92 Gooch; 93 Kapil, Kapil; 94 Atherton, openers; 95 Three celebrations; 96-7 Hat-trick; 98-9 Atherton sequence; 100 Knight; 101 Hussain; 102-3 Streak, Knight, Stewart, Knight; 109 Gooch, Imran, Cozier; 110 Sobers; 111 Lillee, Wasim; 112 Marks, Tendulkar; 113 Richards; 114 Chappell, Botham, poster; 115 Swanton, Greenidge; 118 Agnew; 119 Clark.

ALLSPORT HISTORICAL COLLECTION © HULTON GETTY:

9 Lock family; 14 Laker; 15 Knott; 16 Bailey; 17 England; 19 May, Lindwall; 20 Bailey; 21 Oval, Statham, Tyson, Lock; 23 Trueman; 24 Trueman, Sobers; 25 Barrington, Milburn, Benaud; 26 Shepherd, Lawry, Pollock; 27 Bedsers, Boycott, fans; 29 Packer; 31 Pollock, Packer; 32 Bedi, Gavaskar, Marsh; 33 Holding; 62 Cowdrey & May; 63 Microphone;

64 Ramadhin, Cowdrey; 65 May; 68 Trueman; 69 Trueman, Cowdrey, bath; 79 Willis; 107 Laker; 108 May; 115 Lindwall; 120 Johnners.

PATRICK EAGAR:

Jacket: Lord's action, Arlott, Agnew, Holding; 4 Pigeon; 8 Baxter; 10 Johnston, McGilvray; 15 Gooch; 22 Blofeld; 29 Night cricket, drinks; 30 Richards, Lillee; 31 Thomson; 35 Invasion; 39 SCG; 43 Atherton sequence; 44 Umpire, lights; 50 Trueman; 54 Arlott; 56 Arlott, Johnston; 57 Arlott, 58 Johnston; 59 Arlott; 70 Congdon; 71 Pollard, Congdon; 72 Holding, Greig; 73 West Indies, Amiss; 74-5 Holding sequence; 81 Frindall; 108 Baxter; 110 Knott; 111 Illingworth, Frindall; 112 Lloyd, Bedi; 113 Mosey; 114 Trueman.

GRAHAM MORRIS:

Jacket: Johnston, TMS team; 52 Lloyd; 53 Radio hats; 54 TMS team, CMJ; 56 Museum; 58 Johnston; 80 Frindall, Frindall.

HUGO DIXON:

50 Lunch; 55 Agnew; 81 Scorecard; 110 Fowler.

S&G/ALPHA:

66-7 Cowdrey sequence.

POPPERFOTO:

47 Moore; 61 Rix; 105 Ayckbourn; 116 Carmichael.

· QUIZ ANSWERS ·

1   John Goddard, Sonny Ramadhin and Roy Gilchrist (Headingley 1957).

2   Tony Lock (34 wickets) and Jim Laker (17) versus New Zealand in 1958. (Laker missed one Test.)

3   Ken Mackay (c. O'Neill, at The Oval in 1961).

4   Peter van der Merwe (1965).

5   Derek Underwood (10 for 82 at Headingley in 1972 – Fusarium fungus affected the pitch).

6   David Steele (at Lord's – he made 50 and 45 against Lillee and Thomson).

7   Mike Brearley.

8   Malcolm Marshall (at Headingley in 1984; his left thumb had been broken).

9   Graham Gooch (out for 133 at Old Trafford).

10   Michael Atherton (Lord's 1993 and Headingley 1994).